Pointers in C: A Formula Handbook

N.B. Singh

DEDICATION

To Nature,

I dedicate this book to you, the source of all life. You are my inspiration, my teacher, and my friend.

Thank you for teaching me about the beauty of the world around me. Thank you for showing me the power of the natural world. Thank you for giving me a sense of peace and tranquillity.

I promise to do my part to protect you and your many wonders. I will teach my children about the importance of conservation and sustainability. I will work to make the world a better place for all living things.

Thank you for everything, Nature.

With love,

N.B Singh

Contents

Preface

Welcome to "Pointers in C: A Formula Handbook." This handbook is designed to serve as a comprehensive guide to understanding and mastering the use of pointers in the C programming language.

Why Pointers?

Pointers are a powerful and fundamental concept in C programming, offering a level of flexibility and control over memory that few other features provide. They allow you to work with memory addresses directly, enabling efficient memory management, dynamic data structures, and intricate algorithms.

Who Is This Book For?

This book is intended for C programmers at all levels, from beginners to experienced developers. Whether you are just starting with C or looking to deepen your understanding of pointers, this handbook provides a formulaic approach to grasp the intricacies of pointer manipulation.

Key Features

- **Formulaic Approach:** The content is presented in a formula handbook style, providing concise and practical formulas for common pointer operations.

- **Real-World Examples:** Each formula is accompanied by real-world examples and working code snippets to illustrate its application.

- **In-Depth Coverage:** The book covers a wide range of pointer-related topics, including pointer arithmetic, dynamic memory allocation, pointers to functions, linked lists, and more.

- **Quick Reference:** A quick reference section at the end summarizes key pointer syntax and operations for easy and quick access.

How to Use This Book

The handbook is organized into chapters, each focusing on a specific aspect of pointers. You can use it as a step-by-step guide or as a quick reference for specific topics. Each chapter contains formulas, examples, and explanations to ensure a comprehensive understanding.

Thank you for choosing "Pointers in C: A Formula Handbook." Happy coding!

Chapter 1

Introduction to Pointers

1.1 Overview of Pointers

Pointers in C provide a powerful mechanism for manipulating memory and data. A pointer is a variable that stores the address of another variable. Understanding pointers is crucial for effective C programming. This section provides an overview of key concepts related to pointers.

1.1.1 Basic Concepts

In C, every variable is stored in a specific memory location. A pointer, therefore, is a variable that stores the memory address of another variable. It allows us to indirectly access and modify the data stored in that memory location.

1.1.2 Pointer Syntax

The syntax for declaring a pointer involves specifying the data type it points to, followed by an asterisk (*). For example:

```
int *ptr; // Declares a pointer to an integer
char *charPtr; // Declares a pointer to a character
```

1.1.3 Pointer Arithmetic

Pointer arithmetic involves manipulating pointers using addition or subtraction operations. For example:

```
int numbers[] = {1, 2, 3, 4, 5};
int *ptr = numbers; // Pointer points to the first element


// Accessing elements using pointer arithmetic
int thirdElement = *(ptr + 2); // Accesses the third element (3)
```

Understanding these fundamental concepts sets the stage for exploring more advanced aspects of pointers in C.

1.2 Basic Concepts

Understanding the basic concepts of pointers is essential for proficient C programming. Let's delve into some fundamental concepts:

1.2.1 Memory Address and Variables

In C, every variable is associated with a memory address. A pointer is a variable that holds the memory address of another variable. Consider the following declaration:

```
int number = 42;
int *ptr = &number; // Pointer pointing to the address of 'number'
```

Here, ptr holds the memory address of the number variable.

1.2.2 Dereferencing Pointers

Dereferencing a pointer means accessing the value stored at the memory address it points to. The unary operator * is used for dereferencing. For example:

```
int value = *ptr; // 'value' now holds the value stored at the address in 'ptr'
```

1.2.3 Null Pointers

A null pointer is a pointer that does not point to any memory location. It is often used to indicate that the pointer is not intended to point to a valid object. For instance:

```
int *nullPtr = NULL; // 'nullPtr' is a null pointer
```

1.2.4 Pointer Arithmetic

Pointers support arithmetic operations, making it possible to navigate through memory locations. For example:

```
int numbers[] = {1, 2, 3, 4, 5};
int *ptr = numbers;


// Accessing array elements using pointer arithmetic
int thirdElement = *(ptr + 2); // 'thirdElement' is now 3
```

These concepts provide a foundation for exploring more advanced features of pointers in C.

1.3 Pointer Syntax

Understanding the syntax of pointers is crucial for working with them in C. Let's explore the key aspects:

1.3.1 Declaration and Initialization

In C, pointers are declared by specifying the data type they point to, followed by an asterisk (*). Here's an example:

```
int number = 42;
int *ptr; // Declaration of a pointer to an integer
ptr = &number; // Initialization with the address of 'number'
```

In this example, `ptr` is a pointer to an integer.

1.3.2 Pointer to Different Data Types

Pointers can be declared to point to different data types. For instance:

```
double pi = 3.14159;
double *piPtr = &pi; // Pointer to a double
```

Here, `piPtr` is a pointer to a double.

1.3.3 Pointer Arithmetic

Pointer arithmetic involves manipulating pointers using addition or subtraction. Consider an array example:

```
int numbers[] = {1, 2, 3, 4, 5};
int *ptr = numbers; // Pointer points to the first element


// Accessing elements using pointer arithmetic
int thirdElement = *(ptr + 2); // Accesses the third element (3)
```

In this case, `ptr` is incremented by 2 to access the third element.

1.3.4 Pointer to Functions

Pointers can also point to functions, allowing for dynamic function calls. Here's a basic example:

```
void greet() {
    printf("Hello, World!\n");
}


void (*functionPtr)() = greet; // Pointer to the 'greet' function
```

Now, `functionPtr` points to the `greet` function.

Understanding these syntax elements is essential for effectively utilizing pointers in C.

1.4   Pointer Syntax

Understanding the syntax of pointers is crucial for working with them in C. Let's explore the key aspects:

1.4.1   Declaration and Initialization

In C, pointers are declared by specifying the data type they point to, followed by an asterisk (*). Here's an example:

```
int number = 42;
int *ptr; // Declaration of a pointer to an integer
ptr = &number; // Initialization with the address of 'number'
```

In this example, `ptr` is a pointer to an integer.

1.4.2   Pointer to Different Data Types

Pointers can be declared to point to different data types. For instance:

```
double pi = 3.14159;
double *piPtr = &pi; // Pointer to a double
```

Here, `piPtr` is a pointer to a double.

1.4.3   Pointer Arithmetic

Pointer arithmetic involves manipulating pointers using addition or subtraction. Consider an array example:

```
int numbers[] = {1, 2, 3, 4, 5};
int *ptr = numbers; // Pointer points to the first element


// Accessing elements using pointer arithmetic
int thirdElement = *(ptr + 2); // Accesses the third element (3)
```

In this case, `ptr` is incremented by 2 to access the third element.

1.4.4   Pointer to Functions

Pointers can also point to functions, allowing for dynamic function calls. Here's a basic example:

```
void greet() {
    printf("Hello, World!\n");
}


void (*functionPtr)() = greet; // Pointer to the 'greet' function
```

Now, `functionPtr` points to the `greet` function.

Understanding these syntax elements is essential for effectively utilizing pointers in C.

Chapter 2

Pointer Types and Declarations

2.1 Pointers to Different Data Types

In C, pointers are versatile and can be used to point to different data types. Let's explore the nuances of pointers with various data types:

2.1.1 Pointers to Integers

Pointers can be declared to point to integers. Consider the following example:

```
int num = 42;
int *intPtr = &num; // Pointer to an integer
```

Here, `intPtr` holds the memory address of the integer `num`.

2.1.2 Pointers to Doubles

Similarly, pointers can be used with double data types:

```
double pi = 3.14159;
double *doublePtr = &pi; // Pointer to a double
```

Now, `doublePtr` points to the double variable `pi`.

2.1.3   Pointers to Characters

Pointers can also point to characters:

```
char letter = 'A';
char *charPtr = &letter; // Pointer to a character
```

`charPtr` holds the address of the character variable `letter`.

2.1.4   Pointers to Arrays

Arrays and pointers have a close relationship in C. Pointers can be used to point to arrays of various data types:

```
int numbers[] = {1, 2, 3, 4, 5};
int *arrPtr = numbers; // Pointer to the first element of the array
```

Now, `arrPtr` points to the first element of the integer array `numbers`.

2.1.5   Pointers to Structures

Pointers can also point to structures:

```
struct Point {
    int x;
    int y;
};


struct Point p = {3, 4};
struct Point *structPtr = &p; // Pointer to a structure
```

Here, `structPtr` holds the address of the structure variable p.

2.1.6 Void Pointers

A void pointer is a special type of pointer that can point to objects of any data type. It provides flexibility but requires careful typecasting:

```
void *genericPtr;
int num = 10;
genericPtr = &num; // Assigning address of an integer
```

Using void pointers allows for more dynamic memory allocation and generic functions.

2.1.7 Pointer Typecasting

When working with void pointers, typecasting is necessary to access the data. For example:

```
void *genericPtr;
int num = 10;
genericPtr = &num; // Assigning address of an integer

// Typecasting to access the value
int value = *((int*)genericPtr);
```

Typecasting ensures proper interpretation of the data pointed to by the void pointer.

Understanding these different types of pointers is crucial for efficient and flexible programming in C.

2.2 Pointer Declarations and Initialization

Proper declaration and initialization of pointers are crucial in C programming. Let's explore the syntax and examples for declaring and initializing pointers:

2.2.1   Basic Pointer Declaration

A pointer in C is declared by specifying the data type it points to, followed by an asterisk (*):

```
int *intPtr; // Pointer to an integer
```

Here, `intPtr` is declared as a pointer to an integer.

2.2.2   Pointer Initialization

Pointers should be initialized with the memory address of a variable before they are used:

```
int num = 42;
int *ptr = &num; // Pointer initialized with the address of 'num'
```

Now, `ptr` holds the memory address of the integer variable `num`.

2.2.3   Null Pointers

Pointers can be explicitly set to null, indicating that they are not pointing to any valid memory address:

```
int *nullPtr = NULL; // 'nullPtr' is a null pointer
```

Null pointers are commonly used to signify that the pointer is not currently pointing to any valid data.

2.2.4   Multiple Pointer Declarations

Multiple pointers can be declared in a single line:

```
int *ptr1, *ptr2; // Declares two pointers to integers
```

Both `ptr1` and `ptr2` are now pointers to integers.

2.2.5 Constant Pointers

Pointers can be declared as constant, meaning that the address they point to cannot be changed:

```
int num = 10;
const int *constPtr = &num; // Constant pointer to an integer
```

Here, `constPtr` is a constant pointer to an integer.

2.2.6 Arrays and Pointers

Arrays and pointers are closely related in C. The name of an array is essentially a pointer to its first element:

```
int numbers[] = {1, 2, 3, 4, 5};
int *arrPtr = numbers; // 'arrPtr' points to the first element of 'numbers'
```

Understanding the correct syntax for pointer declarations and initializations is essential for avoiding errors and ensuring proper memory access in C.

2.2.7 Function Pointers

Pointers can also be used to point to functions. The syntax for declaring a function pointer involves specifying the return type and parameter types of the function it can point to:

```
int add(int a, int b) {
    return a + b;
}


int (*funcPtr)(int, int) = add; // 'funcPtr' points to the 'add' function
```

Now, `funcPtr` is a pointer to a function that takes two integers and returns an integer.

2.2.8   Pointer to Void

A pointer to void is a generic pointer that can be used to point to objects of any data type:

```
void *genericPtr;
int num = 20;
genericPtr = &num; // 'genericPtr' points to an integer
```

Careful typecasting is required when dereferencing void pointers.

2.2.9   Dynamic Memory Allocation

Pointers play a crucial role in dynamic memory allocation using functions like `malloc()` and `free()`:

```
int *dynamicPtr = (int *)malloc(sizeof(int));
// Allocates memory for an integer
*dynamicPtr = 30; // Assigns a value to the dynamically allocated memory
free(dynamicPtr); // Releases the allocated memory
```

Understanding dynamic memory allocation is essential for managing memory efficiently in C.

2.2.10   Pointers to Structures

Structures in C can be accessed using pointers, providing a way to navigate through complex data structures:

```
struct Point {
    int x;
    int y;
};

struct Point p = {5, 8};
struct Point *structPtr = &p; // 'structPtr' points to the structure 'p'
```

Now, `structPtr` can be used to access the members of the structure p.

2.2.11 Pointer to Pointers

Pointers to pointers, also known as double pointers, add another layer of indirection:

```
int num = 15;
int *ptr = &num;
int **doublePtr = &ptr; // 'doublePtr' is a pointer to a pointer
```

Double pointers are often used in scenarios where modifying the original pointer is necessary.

2.2.12 Pointer Arithmetic

Pointer arithmetic involves manipulating pointers using addition or subtraction, allowing efficient traversal of arrays:

```
int numbers[] = {1, 2, 3, 4, 5};
int *ptr = numbers; // Pointer points to the first element


// Accessing elements using pointer arithmetic
int thirdElement = *(ptr + 2); // Accesses the third element (3)
```

Pointer arithmetic simplifies array manipulation and traversal.

2.2.13 Pointers in Strings

Strings in C are often represented using pointers, providing efficient ways to handle and manipulate character arrays:

```
char str[] = "Pointer";
char *strPtr = str; // 'strPtr' points to the first character of 'str'
```

Now, `strPtr` can be used for string operations.

2.2.14   Function Pointers and Callbacks

Function pointers are powerful tools for implementing callbacks, allowing functions to be passed as arguments:

```
void performOperation(int a, int b, int (*operation)(int, int)) {
    int result = operation(a, b);
    printf("Result: %d\n", result);
}


int add(int a, int b) {
    return a + b;
}


int subtract(int a, int b) {
    return a - b;
}


int main() {
    performOperation(5, 3, add);       // Calls 'add' function
    performOperation(8, 4, subtract); // Calls 'subtract' function
    return 0;
}
```

Here, `performOperation` accepts a function pointer as an argument, allowing different operations to be performed.

2.2.15   Pointers and Multidimensional Arrays

Pointers can be used to navigate through multidimensional arrays, providing a more flexible approach:

```
int matrix[3][3] = {{1, 2, 3}, {4, 5, 6}, {7, 8, 9}};
int *matrixPtr = &matrix[0][0]; // 'matrixPtr' points to the first element
```

```
// Accessing elements using pointer arithmetic
int fifthElement = *(matrixPtr + 4); // Accesses the fifth element (5)
```

This approach simplifies working with arrays of varying dimensions.

2.2.16 File Handling with Pointers

Pointers are often employed in file handling operations, allowing efficient reading and writing of data:

```
FILE *filePtr;
filePtr = fopen("example.txt", "w"); // Opens a file for writing


if (filePtr != NULL) {
    fprintf(filePtr, "Hello, File!");
    fclose(filePtr); // Closes the file
}
```

Pointers streamline file operations, providing a direct interface with memory.

2.2.17 Error Handling with Pointers

Effective error handling with pointers is essential for robust C programming. Checking for null pointers after dynamic memory allocation is a common practice:

```
int *dynamicPtr = (int *)malloc(sizeof(int));


if (dynamicPtr == NULL) {
    fprintf(stderr, "Memory allocation failed");
    exit(EXIT_FAILURE);
}
```

This approach ensures the program gracefully handles memory allocation failures.

2.2.18   Best Practices for Pointer Usage

Understanding best practices is crucial for writing maintainable and bug-free code with pointers. Key practices include:

- **Initialize Pointers:** Always initialize pointers before using them to avoid undefined behavior. - **Check for Null:** Verify that a pointer is not null before dereferencing to prevent segmentation faults. - **Free Dynamically Allocated Memory:** Properly release dynamically allocated memory using `free()` to prevent memory leaks. - **Use const Correctly:** Utilize the `const` keyword to indicate immutability where appropriate, improving code readability. - **Avoid Dangling Pointers:** Be cautious when using pointers to local variables to prevent them from becoming dangling pointers.

2.2.19   Common Pitfalls and How to Avoid Them

Despite their power, pointers can introduce challenges if not used carefully. Common pitfalls include:

- **Dangling Pointers:** Pointers that reference deallocated memory can lead to undefined behavior. Avoid using pointers after the referenced memory has been freed. - **Memory Leaks:** Failing to release dynamically allocated memory can result in memory leaks. Always free memory when it is no longer needed. - **Uninitialized Pointers:** Using uninitialized pointers can lead to unpredictable behavior. Initialize pointers before use to prevent unexpected results. - **Incorrect Pointer Arithmetic:** Mistakes in pointer arithmetic can cause memory access violations. Be meticulous when performing pointer arithmetic and ensure it aligns with the data type.

Understanding these best practices and pitfalls is vital for mastering pointers in C and writing reliable and efficient code.

2.3 Pointers and Arrays

Pointers and arrays in C are closely connected, and understanding their relationship is fundamental. Let's explore the intricacies of using pointers with arrays:

2.3.1 Arrays and Pointers Relationship

In C, the name of an array is essentially a pointer to its first element. Consider the following example:

```
int numbers[] = {1, 2, 3, 4, 5};
int *arrPtr = numbers; // 'arrPtr' points to the first element of 'numbers'
```

Here, arrPtr holds the memory address of the first element of the array numbers.

2.3.2 Accessing Array Elements using Pointers

Pointers offer an alternative way to access array elements. Using pointer arithmetic, we can navigate through the array:

```
int numbers[] = {1, 2, 3, 4, 5};
int *ptr = numbers; // 'ptr' points to the first element

// Accessing elements using pointer arithmetic
int thirdElement = *(ptr + 2); // Accesses the third element (3)
```

The expression *(ptr + 2) is equivalent to accessing the third element of the array.

2.3.3 Pointer Arithmetic with Arrays

Pointer arithmetic provides an efficient means of traversing arrays. Consider the following example:

```
int numbers[] = {1, 2, 3, 4, 5};
int *ptr = numbers; // 'ptr' points to the first element


// Using pointer arithmetic to iterate through the array
for (int i = 0; i < 5; i++) {
    printf("%d ", *ptr);
    ptr++; // Incrementing the pointer to move to the next element
}
```

This loop prints each element of the array using pointer arithmetic for efficient traversal.

2.3.4   Pointers and Multidimensional Arrays

The relationship between pointers and arrays extends to multidimensional arrays. Consider a 2D array:

```
int matrix[3][3] = {{1, 2, 3}, {4, 5, 6}, {7, 8, 9}};
int *matrixPtr = &matrix[0][0]; // 'matrixPtr' points to the first element


// Accessing elements using pointer arithmetic
int fifthElement = *(matrixPtr + 4); // Accesses the fifth element (5)
```

Here, matrixPtr allows us to navigate through the elements of the 2D array.

2.3.5   Arrays of Pointers

Arrays can also store pointers, providing flexibility in managing different data types:

```
int num1 = 10, num2 = 20, num3 = 30;
int *numArray[] = {&num1, &num2, &num3}; // Array of pointers to integers
```

Now, numArray is an array of pointers, each pointing to an integer.

2.3.6 Pointers as Function Arguments

Pointers are often used as function parameters to manipulate arrays directly.
Consider a function to double each element of an array:

```
void doubleArray(int *arr, int size) {
    for (int i = 0; i < size; i++) {
        arr[i] *= 2;
    }
}


int main() {
    int numbers[] = {1, 2, 3, 4, 5};
    doubleArray(numbers, 5); // Doubles each element of 'numbers'
    // 'numbers' now contains {2, 4, 6, 8, 10}
    return 0;
}
```

Here, `doubleArray` takes a pointer to an integer array as an argument.

2.3.7 Pointers and Strings

Strings in C are typically represented as character arrays, and pointers simplify
string manipulations:

```
char str[] = "Pointer";
char *strPtr = str; // 'strPtr' points to the first character of 'str'
```

Now, `strPtr` can be used for various string operations.

2.3.8 Dynamic Memory Allocation for Arrays

Pointers play a crucial role in dynamic memory allocation for arrays. Here's an
example:

```
int *dynamicArray = (int *)malloc(5 * sizeof(int));
// Allocates memory for an integer array


// Accessing and modifying elements of the dynamically allocated array
dynamicArray[2] = 42;
free(dynamicArray); // Releases the allocated memory
```

Dynamic memory allocation allows for flexibility in managing arrays of varying sizes.

2.3.9   Arrays of Pointers to Strings

Arrays of pointers are commonly used to handle arrays of strings:

```
char *colors[] = {"Red", "Green", "Blue"};
```

Now, colors is an array of pointers, each pointing to a different string.

2.3.10   Function Pointers and Arrays

Arrays of function pointers allow for dynamic invocation of functions. Consider the following:

```
int add(int a, int b) {
    return a + b;
}


int subtract(int a, int b) {
    return a - b;
}


// Array of function pointers
int (*operations[2])(int, int) = {add, subtract};
```

```
int main() {
    int result = operations[0](5, 3); // Invokes the 'add' function
    return 0;
}
```

Here, `operations` is an array of function pointers, providing a way to dynamically choose and invoke functions.

2.3.11 Error Handling with Arrays and Pointers

Proper error handling is crucial when working with arrays and pointers. For example, checking for array bounds:

```
int numbers[] = {1, 2, 3, 4, 5};
int index = 7;


if (index >= 0 && index < sizeof(numbers) / sizeof(numbers[0])) {
    int value = numbers[index];
    // Proceed with using 'value'
} else {
    // Handle out-of-bounds error
}
```

This ensures that array indices are within bounds, preventing memory access violations.

2.3.12 Pointers to Pointers and Arrays

Pointers to pointers (double pointers) are valuable in managing arrays of pointers, providing an additional layer of indirection:

```
int num1 = 10, num2 = 20, num3 = 30;
int *ptr1 = &num1, *ptr2 = &num2, *ptr3 = &num3;
```

```
// Array of pointers
int *ptrArray[] = {ptr1, ptr2, ptr3};
// Double pointer pointing to the array of pointers
int **doublePtr = ptrArray;
```

Now, `doublePtr` points to the array of pointers, offering a flexible structure.

2.3.13   Best Practices for Pointers and Arrays

Understanding best practices ensures the effective use of pointers and arrays in C:

- **Avoid Pointer Arithmetic Pitfalls:** Be cautious when using pointer arithmetic to avoid out-of-bounds access or undefined behavior. - **Initialize Pointers Properly:** Always initialize pointers before use to prevent accidental dereferencing of uninitialized pointers. - **Use `const` for Immutable Arrays:** When applicable, use the `const` keyword to indicate that an array is immutable, enhancing code clarity. - **Free Dynamically Allocated Memory:** Properly release dynamically allocated memory for arrays to prevent memory leaks. - **Use `sizeof` for Array Sizes:** Utilize `sizeof` to calculate the size of arrays dynamically, ensuring portability and avoiding hardcoding sizes.

2.3.14   Common Pitfalls and How to Avoid Them

Despite their power, pointers and arrays can introduce challenges if not used carefully. Common pitfalls include:

- **Out-of-Bounds Access:** Be mindful of array bounds to prevent out-of-bounds access, which can lead to undefined behavior. - **Dangling Pointers:** Avoid using pointers after the referenced memory has been freed, as this can result in dangling pointers. - **Memory Leaks:** Always free dynamically allocated memory to prevent memory leaks and ensure efficient memory usage. - **Confusing Pointers with Arrays:** Understand the difference between pointers and arrays to avoid confusion in their usage. - **Incorrect Array Initialization:** Properly initialize arrays to avoid unexpected values or behavior in array operations.

Understanding these best practices and pitfalls is vital for mastering the effective use of pointers and arrays in C programming.

2.4 Pointers to Functions

Pointers to functions in C allow for dynamic function invocation and enhance flexibility in program design. Let's explore the syntax and examples of using pointers to functions:

2.4.1 Basic Syntax for Function Pointers

The syntax for declaring a pointer to a function involves specifying the return type and parameter types of the function it can point to:

```
int add(int a, int b) {
    return a + b;
}


// Declaration of a function pointer for 'add'
int (*funcPtr)(int, int) = add;
```

Here, funcPtr is a pointer to a function that takes two integers and returns an integer.

2.4.2 Function Pointer Invocation

Using a function pointer involves invoking the function it points to, just like a regular function call:

```
int result = funcPtr(3, 5); // Invokes the 'add' function through the pointer
```

The variable result now holds the value returned by the add function.

2.4.3   Function Pointers as Parameters

Function pointers can be passed as parameters to functions, providing a mechanism for dynamic behavior:

```
int add(int a, int b) {
    return a + b;
}


int subtract(int a, int b) {
    return a - b;
}


int performOperation(int x, int y, int (*operation)(int, int)) {
    return operation(x, y);
}


int result1 = performOperation(5, 3, add);      // Invokes 'add'
int result2 = performOperation(8, 4, subtract); // Invokes 'subtract'
```

Here, performOperation accepts a function pointer as an argument, allowing different operations to be performed dynamically.

2.4.4   Arrays of Function Pointers

Arrays of function pointers provide a convenient way to manage multiple functions:

```
int add(int a, int b) {
    return a + b;
}


int subtract(int a, int b) {
    return a - b;
```

```
}
```

```
// Array of function pointers
int (*operations[2])(int, int) = {add, subtract};
```

```
int result = operations[0](5, 3); // Invokes 'add' through the array
```

Here, `operations` is an array of function pointers, allowing for dynamic selection and invocation of functions.

2.4.5 Function Pointers and Callbacks

Function pointers are often used in scenarios where functions need to be passed as arguments, enabling callback functionality:

```
void performOperation(int a, int b, int (*operation)(int, int)) {
    int result = operation(a, b);
    printf("Result: %d\n", result);
}
```

```
int add(int a, int b) {
    return a + b;
}
```

```
int subtract(int a, int b) {
    return a - b;
}
```

```
int main() {
    performOperation(5, 3, add);      // Calls 'add' function
    performOperation(8, 4, subtract); // Calls 'subtract' function
    return 0;
}
```

In this example, `performOperation` accepts a function pointer as a callback, allowing different operations to be performed based on user input.

2.4.6   Pointers to Functions in Structures

Structures can contain function pointers, providing a way to organize related functions:

```
struct MathOperations {
    int (*add)(int, int);
    int (*subtract)(int, int);
};


struct MathOperations mathOps = {add, subtract};


int result = mathOps.add(5, 3); // Invokes 'add' through the structure
```

Here, `mathOps` is a structure containing function pointers, allowing for a cohesive organization of related functions.

2.4.7   Dynamic Function Selection

Function pointers enable dynamic selection of functions at runtime, leading to more adaptable and modular code:

```
int square(int x) {
    return x * x;
}


int cube(int x) {
    return x * x * x;
}


int dynamicOperation(int x, int (*func)(int)) {
```

```
    return func(x);
}


int result1 = dynamicOperation(4, square); // Squares the number
int result2 = dynamicOperation(3, cube);   // Cubes the number
```

The `dynamicOperation` function dynamically selects and invokes the specified function.

2.4.8 Function Pointers in Sorting Algorithms

Function pointers are commonly used in sorting algorithms, allowing the algorithm to be more versatile:

```
#include <stdio.h>
#include <stdlib.h>


int compareAscending(const void *a, const void *b) {
    return (*(int *)a - *(int *)b);
}


int compareDescending(const void *a, const void *b) {
    return (*(int *)b - *(int *)a);
}


int main() {
    int arr[] = {4, 2, 7, 1, 9, 5};

    // Sorting in ascending order
    qsort(arr, 6, sizeof(int), compareAscending);

    // Sorting in descending order
```

```
    qsort(arr, 6, sizeof(int), compareDescending);

    return 0;
}
```

In this example, `qsort` uses function pointers (`compareAscending` and `compareDescending`) to dynamically determine the sorting order.

2.4.9   Pointers to Variadic Functions

Function pointers can be used with variadic functions, allowing for flexibility in handling variable arguments:

```
#include <stdarg.h>
#include <stdio.h>

int sum(int count, ...) {
    va_list args;
    va_start(args, count);

    int result = 0;
    for (int i = 0; i < count; i++) {
        result += va_arg(args, int);
    }

    va_end(args);
    return result;
}

int main() {
    int total = sum(3, 5, 8, 12); // Sums the three provided numbers
    return 0;
}
```

Here, `sum` is a variadic function, and a function pointer could be used to point to it.

2.4.10 Function Pointers and Callback Mechanisms

Callback mechanisms in event-driven programming often utilize function pointers to handle specific events:

```
typedef void (*EventHandler)(void);
```

```
void buttonClicked() {
    printf("Button clicked!\n");
}
```

```
void registerEvent(EventHandler eventHandler) {
    // Some registration logic
    eventHandler(); // Callback the registered event handler
}
```

```
int main() {
    registerEvent(buttonClicked); // Registers the button click event
    return 0;
}
```

In this example, `buttonClicked` serves as a callback function registered to handle a specific event.

2.4.11 Error Handling with Function Pointers

Function pointers can enhance error handling by providing a mechanism for custom error-handling functions:

```
#include <stdio.h>
```

```c
void handleDefaultError() {
    fprintf(stderr, "An error occurred.\n");
}


void performOperation(int a, int b,
int (*operation)(int, int), void (*errorHandler)()) {
    if (operation != NULL) {
        int result = operation(a, b);
        printf("Result: %d\n", result);
    } else {
        if (errorHandler != NULL) {
            errorHandler();
        }
    }
}


int main() {
    performOperation(5, 0, divide, handleDefaultError);
    return 0;
}
```

In this example, `performOperation` includes an error-handling function pointer, allowing customization of error-handling behavior.

2.4.12   Best Practices for Function Pointers

Effectively using function pointers requires adherence to best practices:

- **Null-Check Function Pointers:** Always check if a function pointer is not null before invoking it to avoid undefined behavior. - **Use Typedefs for Complex Signatures:** When dealing with complex function signatures, use `typedefs` to improve code readability. - **Document Function Pointer Signatures:** Clearly document the expected function signatures when using function pointers, promoting code understandability. - **Avoid Dangling Function Pointers:** Ensure that function pointers do not outlive the functions they point to by managing their scope appropriately. - **Consider Using Function Pointers in Structs:** For related functions, consider organizing them within structures using function pointers.

2.4.13 Common Pitfalls with Function Pointers

Mistakes with function pointers can lead to errors and unexpected behavior. Common pitfalls include:

- **Mismatched Function Signatures:** Ensure that function pointer signatures match the functions they point to; otherwise, undefined behavior may occur. - **Null Function Pointers:** Avoid dereferencing null function pointers, as it leads to unpredictable results. - **Incorrect Use of Typedefs:** Be consistent and accurate when using `typedefs` for function pointer types to prevent confusion.

Understanding these best practices and pitfalls is essential for mastering function pointers in C programming.

Chapter 3

Dynamic Memory Allocation

3.1 Memory Management in C

Memory management is a critical aspect of programming in C, and understanding dynamic memory allocation is crucial for efficient and flexible memory usage. This section explores the concepts and techniques related to memory management in C.

3.1.1 Dynamic Memory Allocation Basics

In C, dynamic memory allocation is performed using the 'malloc' function from the 'stdlib.h' library. The general syntax is:

$$ptr = (type*)malloc(size)$$

Here, ptr is a pointer of type type*, and size is the number of bytes to allocate. For example:

$$int *arr = (int*)malloc(5 * sizeof(int))$$

This allocates memory for an array of 5 integers.

3.1.2 Memory Deallocation with free()

Memory allocated using 'malloc' must be released to prevent memory leaks. The 'free' function is used for this purpose:

$$free(ptr)$$

Here, ptr is the pointer to the memory to be deallocated.

3.1.3 calloc and realloc Functions

The 'calloc' function allocates memory for an array of elements, initializing them to zero. Its syntax is similar to 'malloc':

$$ptr = (type*)calloc(num\_elements, sizeof(type))$$

The 'realloc' function is used to resize previously allocated memory:

$$ptr = (type*)realloc(ptr, new\_size)$$

It takes a pointer to previously allocated memory, resizes it to the new size, and returns the new pointer.

3.1.4 Example: Dynamic Array Creation

Consider the following example of dynamically creating an array of integers:

```c
#include <stdio.h>
#include <stdlib.h>

int main() {
    int *dynamicArray;
    int size = 5;
```

```c
    // Allocating memory for an integer array
    dynamicArray = (int*)malloc(size * sizeof(int));

    // Checking if allocation was successful
    if (dynamicArray != NULL) {
        // Initializing the array
        for (int i = 0; i < size; i++) {
            dynamicArray[i] = i * 2;
        }

        // Printing the array
        for (int i = 0; i < size; i++) {
            printf("%d ", dynamicArray[i]);
        }

        // Deallocating memory
        free(dynamicArray);
    } else {
        fprintf(stderr, "Memory allocation failed");
    }

    return 0;
}
```

In this example, memory is allocated for an array of integers, initialized, printed, and then deallocated.

3.1.5 Example: Resizing an Array using realloc

The 'realloc' function allows resizing an array dynamically. Here's an example:

```c
#include <stdio.h>
```

```c
#include <stdlib.h>

int main() {
    int *dynamicArray;
    int initialSize = 5;

    // Allocating memory for an integer array
    dynamicArray = (int*)malloc(initialSize * sizeof(int));

    if (dynamicArray != NULL) {
        // Initializing the array
        for (int i = 0; i < initialSize; i++) {
            dynamicArray[i] = i * 2;
        }

        // Printing the original array
        printf("Original Array: ");
        for (int i = 0; i < initialSize; i++) {
            printf("%d ", dynamicArray[i]);
        }

        // Resizing the array to a larger size
        int newSize = 8;
        dynamicArray = (int*)realloc(dynamicArray, newSize * sizeof(int));

        // Adding new elements to the resized array
        for (int i = initialSize; i < newSize; i++) {
            dynamicArray[i] = i * 2;
        }

        // Printing the resized array
```

```
    printf("\nResized Array: ");
    for (int i = 0; i < newSize; i++) {
        printf("%d ", dynamicArray[i]);
    }


    // Deallocating memory
    free(dynamicArray);
} else {
    fprintf(stderr, "Memory allocation failed");
}


    return 0;
}
```

This example allocates an array, resizes it using 'realloc', adds new elements, and prints the original and resized arrays.

3.1.6   Dynamic Memory for Strings

Dynamic memory allocation is commonly used for strings, where the size may vary during runtime:

```
#include <stdio.h>
#include <stdlib.h>
#include <string.h>

int main() {
    char *dynamicString;

    // Allocating memory for a string
    dynamicString = (char*)malloc(10 * sizeof(char));
```

```c
    if (dynamicString != NULL) {
        // Initializing the string
        strcpy(dynamicString, "Dynamic");

        // Printing the string
        printf("String: %s\n", dynamicString);

        // Deallocating memory
        free(dynamicString);
    } else {
        fprintf(stderr, "Memory allocation failed");
    }


    return 0;
}
```

Here, memory is allocated for a string, initialized, printed, and then deallocated.

3.1.7   Error Handling in Dynamic Memory Allocation

Error handling is essential when working with dynamic memory allocation. Checking if memory allocation was successful helps prevent unexpected behavior:

```c
#include <stdio.h>
#include <stdlib.h>

int main() {
    int *dynamicArray;
    int size = 10;
```

```c
    // Attempting to allocate memory
    dynamicArray = (int*)malloc(size * sizeof(int));

    // Checking if allocation was successful
    if (dynamicArray != NULL) {
        // Memory allocation successful, proceed with usage

        // Deallocating memory
        free(dynamicArray);
    } else {
        fprintf(stderr, "Memory allocation failed");
    }

    return 0;
}
```

This example checks if memory allocation was successful before proceeding with further operations.

3.1.8 Best Practices for Dynamic Memory Allocation

Effective use of dynamic memory in C requires adherence to best practices:

- **Check for NULL After Allocation:** Always check if the memory allocation function returns NULL to avoid dereferencing a null pointer. - **Free Allocated Memory:** Always release dynamically allocated memory using 'free' to prevent memory leaks. - **Use 'calloc' for Zero Initialization:** When initializing memory to zero, consider using 'calloc' for clarity and efficiency. - **Avoid Fragmentation with 'realloc':** Frequent resizing of memory using 'realloc' may lead to fragmentation; use it judiciously. - **Initialize Pointers After Allocation:** Initialize pointers immediately after dynamic memory allocation to avoid using uninitialized memory.

3.1.9   Common Pitfalls in Dynamic Memory Allocation

Mistakes in dynamic memory allocation can lead to runtime errors and memory leaks. Common pitfalls include:

- **Forgetting to Free Memory:** Failing to free dynamically allocated memory leads to memory leaks and potential program instability. - **Dangling Pointers:** Accessing memory through a dangling pointer (after it has been freed) results in undefined behavior. - **Mismatched 'malloc' and 'free':** Ensure that the same memory allocation function ('malloc', 'calloc', or 'realloc') is used with its corresponding 'free' function. - **Failure to Check for NULL:** Neglecting to check for NULL after memory allocation can lead to segmentation faults or other errors.

Understanding these best practices and pitfalls is crucial for effective dynamic memory allocation in C programming.

3.2   malloc(), calloc(), realloc(), and free()

Dynamic memory allocation in C is facilitated by four essential functions: `malloc()`, `calloc()`, `realloc()`, and `free()`. These functions allow programmers to manage memory dynamically during program execution.

3.2.1   malloc() Function

The `malloc()` function, short for "memory allocation," is used to allocate a specified number of bytes in the heap memory. Its general syntax is:

```
ptr = (type*)malloc(size);
```

Here, `ptr` is a pointer of type `type*`, and `size` is the number of bytes to allocate. For example:

```
int *arr = (int*)malloc(5 * sizeof(int));
```

This allocates memory for an array of 5 integers.

3.2.2 calloc() Function

The `calloc()` function, short for "contiguous allocation," is similar to `malloc()` but initializes the allocated memory to zero. Its syntax is:

```
ptr = (type*)calloc(num_elements, sizeof(type));
```

Here, `ptr` is a pointer to the allocated memory, and `num_elements` is the number of elements to allocate. For example:

```
int *arr = (int*)calloc(5, sizeof(int));
```

This allocates memory for an array of 5 integers, initializing them to zero.

3.2.3 realloc() Function

The `realloc()` function, short for "re-allocation," is used to resize previously allocated memory. Its syntax is:

```
ptr = (type*)realloc(ptr, new_size);
```

Here, `ptr` is a pointer to previously allocated memory, and `new_size` is the new size in bytes. For example:

```
int *resizedArr = (int*)realloc(arr, 8 * sizeof(int));
```

This resizes the previously allocated array to accommodate 8 integers.

3.2.4 free() Function

The `free()` function is used to deallocate memory previously allocated using `malloc()`, `calloc()`, or `realloc()`. Its syntax is simple:

```
free(ptr);
```

Here, `ptr` is the pointer to the memory to be deallocated. For example:

```
                    free(arr);
```

This deallocates the memory allocated for the array.

3.2.5   Example: Dynamic Array Creation

Let's explore an example illustrating the use of `malloc()` to dynamically create
an array of integers:

```c
#include <stdio.h>
#include <stdlib.h>

int main() {
    int *dynamicArray;
    int size = 5;

    // Allocating memory for an integer array
    dynamicArray = (int*)malloc(size * sizeof(int));

    // Checking if allocation was successful
    if (dynamicArray != NULL) {
        // Initializing the array
        for (int i = 0; i < size; i++) {
            dynamicArray[i] = i * 2;
        }

        // Printing the array
        for (int i = 0; i < size; i++) {
            printf("%d ", dynamicArray[i]);
        }

        // Deallocating memory
```

```
        free(dynamicArray);
    } else {
        fprintf(stderr, "Memory allocation failed");
    }


    return 0;
}
```

In this example, memory is allocated for an array of integers, initialized, printed, and then deallocated using `free()`.

3.2.6   Example: Resizing an Array using realloc()

Now, let's consider an example demonstrating the use of `realloc()` to resize an array dynamically:

```
#include <stdio.h>
#include <stdlib.h>

int main() {
    int *dynamicArray;
    int initialSize = 5;

    // Allocating memory for an integer array
    dynamicArray = (int*)malloc(initialSize * sizeof(int));

    if (dynamicArray != NULL) {
        // Initializing the array
        for (int i = 0; i < initialSize; i++) {
            dynamicArray[i] = i * 2;
        }
```

```c
    // Printing the original array
    printf("Original Array: ");
    for (int i = 0; i < initialSize; i++) {
        printf("%d ", dynamicArray[i]);
    }


    // Resizing the array to a larger size
    int newSize = 8;
    dynamicArray = (int*)realloc(dynamicArray, newSize * sizeof(int));


    // Adding new elements to the resized array
    for (int i = initialSize; i < newSize; i++) {
        dynamicArray[i] = i * 2;
    }


    // Printing the resized array
    printf("\nResized Array: ");
    for (int i = 0; i < newSize; i++) {
        printf("%d ", dynamicArray[i]);
    }


    // Deallocating memory
    free(dynamicArray);
} else {
    fprintf(stderr, "Memory allocation failed");
}


return 0;
}
```

In this example, an array is initially allocated, resized using `realloc()`, new elements are added, and the resized array is printed.

3.2.7   Numerical Example: Memory Allocation for Matrices

Consider a scenario where a matrix needs to be dynamically allocated. The following code demonstrates this:

```c
#include <stdio.h>
#include <stdlib.h>

int main() {
    int rows = 3, cols = 4;

    // Allocating memory for a 2D array (matrix)
    int **matrix = (int**)malloc(rows * sizeof(int*));

    // Checking if allocation was successful
    if (matrix != NULL) {
        for (int i = 0; i < rows; i++) {
            matrix[i] = (int*)malloc(cols * sizeof(int));
        }

        // Initializing the matrix
        for (int i = 0; i < rows; i++) {
            for (int j = 0; j < cols; j++) {
                matrix[i][j] = i + j;
            }
        }

        // Printing the matrix
        printf("Matrix:\n");
```

```c
    for (int i = 0; i < rows; i++) {
        for (int j = 0; j < cols; j++) {
            printf("%d ", matrix[i][j]);
        }
        printf("\n");
    }


    // Deallocating memory
    for (int i = 0; i < rows; i++) {
        free(matrix[i]);
    }
    free(matrix);
} else {
    fprintf(stderr, "Memory allocation failed");
}


    return 0;
}
```

This example allocates memory for a 3x4 matrix, initializes it, prints the matrix, and then deallocates the memory.

3.2.8   Best Practices for Dynamic Memory Allocation

Effectively using `malloc()`, `calloc()`, `realloc()`, and `free()` requires adherence to best practices:

- **Check for NULL After Allocation:** Always check if the memory allocation function returns NULL to avoid dereferencing a null pointer. - **Free Allocated Memory:** Always release dynamically allocated memory using `free` to prevent memory leaks. - **Use `calloc` for Zero Initialization:** When initializing memory to zero, consider using `calloc` for clarity and efficiency. - **Avoid Fragmentation with `realloc`:** Frequent resizing of memory using `realloc` may lead to fragmentation; use it judiciously. - **Initialize Pointers After Allocation:** Initialize pointers immediately after dynamic memory allocation to avoid using uninitialized memory.

3.2.9 Common Pitfalls in Dynamic Memory Allocation

Mistakes in dynamic memory allocation can lead to runtime errors and memory leaks. Common pitfalls include:

- **Forgetting to Free Memory:** Failing to free dynamically allocated memory leads to memory leaks and potential program instability. - **Dangling Pointers:** Accessing memory through a dangling pointer (after it has been freed) results in undefined behavior. - **Mismatched `malloc` and `free`:** Ensure that the same memory allocation function (`malloc`, `calloc`, or `realloc`) is used with its corresponding `free` function. - **Failure to Check for NULL:** Neglecting to check for NULL after memory allocation can lead to segmentation faults or other errors.

Understanding these best practices and pitfalls is crucial for effective dynamic memory allocation in C programming.

3.3 Memory Leak Detection

Memory leaks can be a significant concern in programs that dynamically allocate memory. A memory leak occurs when allocated memory is not properly deallocated, leading to a gradual consumption of system resources. Detecting and preventing memory leaks is crucial for writing robust and efficient C programs.

3.3.1 Causes of Memory Leaks

Memory leaks can arise from various sources, such as:

1. **Not Freeing Allocated Memory:** Failing to use the `free()` function to release dynamically allocated memory.

2. **Lost Pointers:** Losing all references to allocated memory without deallocating it.

3. **Incorrect Pairing of Allocation Functions:**

Mismatching `malloc()`/`calloc()`/`realloc()` with `free()`.

4. **Premature Deallocation:** Deallocating memory that is still being used.

3.3.2   Memory Leak Detection Tools

Several tools are available for detecting memory leaks in C programs. One commonly used tool is Valgrind. Valgrind is a programming tool for memory debugging, memory leak detection, and profiling. To use Valgrind, a program is executed under its supervision, and Valgrind reports memory-related issues.

3.3.3   Example: Memory Leak Detection with Valgrind

Consider the following example where a memory leak is intentionally introduced:

```c
#include <stdlib.h>

int main() {
    int *dynamicArray = (int*)malloc(5 * sizeof(int));

    // Intentional memory leak by not freeing allocated memory
    // Comment the next line to remove the memory leak
    // free(dynamicArray);

    return 0;
}
```

To detect memory leaks using Valgrind, compile the program and run it with Valgrind:

```
gcc -o memory_leak_detection memory_leak_detection.c
```

```
valgrind --leak-check=full ./memory_leak_detection
```

Valgrind will provide a detailed report indicating the source of the memory leak.

3.3.4 Preventing Memory Leaks

Preventing memory leaks requires adherence to best practices:

1. **Always Free Allocated Memory:** Use `free()` to release memory as soon as it is no longer needed.

2. **Track Allocations and Deallocation:** Keep track of memory allocations and deallocations to ensure a proper match.

3. **Use Tools for Detection:** Employ memory leak detection tools like Valgrind during development.

4. **Automated Testing:** Incorporate automated tests that include memory leak checks.

5. **Review Code:** Regularly review and analyze code to identify potential memory leaks.

3.3.5 Numerical Example: Tracking Memory Leaks

Consider the following scenario where memory is allocated and deallocated in a loop, simulating a common situation in programs:

```
#include <stdlib.h>

int main() {
    for (int i = 0; i < 5; i++) {
        int *dynamicArray = (int*)malloc(10 * sizeof(int));

        // Use dynamicArray for some computation

        // Intentional memory leak by not freeing allocated memory
```

```
    // Comment the next line to remove the memory leak
    // free(dynamicArray);
  }


  return 0;
}
```

Running this program through Valgrind will reveal memory leaks due to not freeing allocated memory within the loop.

3.3.6   Best Practices for Memory Leak Prevention

To prevent memory leaks effectively, follow these best practices:

1. **Familiarize Yourself with Allocation Functions:** Understand the behavior of `malloc()`, `calloc()`, `realloc()`, and `free()`.

2. **Adopt a Coding Standard:** Enforce a coding standard that includes proper memory management practices.

3. **Use RAII (Resource Acquisition Is Initialization):** Leverage RAII principles, associating resource acquisition with object initialization and release with object destruction.

4. **Code Reviews:** Regularly conduct code reviews to identify and address potential memory leaks.

5. **Use Automated Tools:** Employ automated memory leak detection tools during development and testing.

3.3.7   Common Pitfalls in Memory Leak Detection

While addressing memory leaks, be aware of common pitfalls:

1. **False Positives:** Memory leak detection tools may produce false positives, indicating a leak where there is none.

2. **False Negatives:** Tools may miss actual memory leaks, leading to false negatives.

3. **Tool Overhead:** Some memory detection tools introduce overhead, affecting program execution speed.

4. **Complex Leak Scenarios:** Detecting leaks in complex scenarios may require a deeper understanding of the tool's output.

Understanding these considerations is vital for effectively utilizing memory leak detection tools.

3.4 Best Practices for Dynamic Memory Allocation

Dynamic memory allocation in C, while powerful, demands careful practices to ensure efficient memory usage, prevent memory leaks, and enhance program stability. This section outlines best practices for handling dynamic memory in C.

3.4.1 1. Check for NULL After Allocation

Always check if the memory allocation function (`malloc()`, `calloc()`, `realloc()`) returns `NULL`. A failed allocation returns `NULL`, indicating insufficient memory. Failing to check for `NULL` can lead to undefined behavior. For example:

```
int *arr = (int*)malloc(5 * sizeof(int));
if (arr == NULL) {
    fprintf(stderr, "Memory allocation failed");
    // Handle the error or exit the program
}
```

3.4.2 2. Free Allocated Memory

Ensure that every dynamically allocated memory block is released using the `free()` function when it is no longer needed. Failure to do so results in memory leaks. For instance:

```
int *arr = (int*)malloc(5 * sizeof(int));
// Use arr for computations
free(arr); // Release the allocated memory when done
```

3.4.3   3. Use `calloc()` for Zero Initialization

When allocating memory that needs to be initialized to zero, prefer `calloc()` over `malloc()`. `calloc()` initializes the allocated memory to zero, providing clarity and efficiency. Example:

```
int *arr = (int*)calloc(5, sizeof(int)); // Allocates and initializes to zero
```

3.4.4   4. Avoid Fragmentation with `realloc()`

Carefully use `realloc()` to resize allocated memory. Frequent resizing may lead to memory fragmentation. It is advisable to allocate memory in larger chunks initially, if possible, to reduce the need for frequent resizing. Example:

```
int *arr = (int*)malloc(5 * sizeof(int));
// Perform computations
arr = (int*)realloc(arr, 10 * sizeof(int)); // Resize to a larger chunk
```

3.4.5   5. Initialize Pointers After Allocation

Immediately initialize pointers after dynamic memory allocation to prevent the use of uninitialized memory. Accessing uninitialized memory leads to undefined behavior. For example:

```
int *arr = (int*)malloc(5 * sizeof(int));
if (arr != NULL) {
    // Initialize the array elements
    // ...
}
```

3.4.6 6. Use `sizeof` for Type-Safe Allocation

Prevent allocation errors by using `sizeof` with the type of the variable. This ensures type safety and avoids hardcoding sizes. Example:

```
int *arr = (int*)malloc(5 * sizeof(int)); // Good practice
int *arr = (int*)malloc(5 * sizeof(int)); // Avoid, as it's less type-safe
```

3.4.7 7. Document Ownership and Lifespan

Clearly document the ownership and expected lifespan of dynamically allocated memory. This helps avoid unintended deallocation or reference issues. Example:

```
// Documenting ownership and lifespan
int *createArray() {
    int *arr = (int*)malloc(5 * sizeof(int));
    // ...
    return arr;
}


void processArray(int *arr) {
    // ...
    free(arr); // Documenting that the responsibility of freeing lies here
}
```

3.4.8 8. Use `calloc()` for Arrays of Structures

When allocating memory for an array of structures, prefer `calloc()` over `malloc()` to ensure zero initialization of each structure. Example:

```
struct Point {
    int x;
    int y;
};
```

```
struct Point *points = (struct Point*)calloc(5, sizeof(struct Point));
```

3.4.9   9. Clear Pointers After Freeing

After freeing dynamically allocated memory, set the pointer to `NULL`. This prevents accidental use of a dangling pointer. Example:

```
int *arr = (int*)malloc(5 * sizeof(int));
// ...
free(arr);
arr = NULL; // Set the pointer to NULL after freeing
```

3.4.10   10. Use `size_t` for Memory Sizes

Prefer using `size_t` for representing sizes of memory blocks. This type is specifically designed for this purpose and can accommodate large sizes. Example:

```
size_t size = 10 * sizeof(int);
int *arr = (int*)malloc(size);
```

3.4.11   11. Test for Memory Leaks

Regularly test your programs for memory leaks using tools like Valgrind. Automated tests focused on memory leak detection can catch issues early in the development process.

3.4.12   12. Avoid Memory Leaks in Error Paths

Ensure that your error-handling paths do not result in memory leaks. Always free any allocated memory before exiting due to an error. Example:

```
int *arr = (int*)malloc(5 * sizeof(int));
if (arr == NULL) {
    fprintf(stderr, "Memory allocation failed");
```

```
    free(arr); // Freeing memory in error path
    exit(EXIT_FAILURE);
}
```

3.4.13   13. Use `realloc()` Carefully

Be cautious when using `realloc()` in scenarios where reallocation might fail. It is essential to check the return value and handle failure appropriately. Example:

```
int *arr = (int*)malloc(5 * sizeof(int));
int *resizedArr = (int*)realloc(arr, 10 * sizeof(int));


if (resizedArr == NULL) {
    fprintf(stderr, "Memory reallocation failed");
    // Handle the failure, possibly free(arr) to avoid memory leak
}
```

3.4.14   14. Avoid Unnecessary Dynamic Allocation

Reserve dynamic memory allocation for situations where it is truly necessary. In some cases, static allocation or automatic variables may be more appropriate.

3.4.15   15. Use `memcpy()` for Memory Copying

When copying data between dynamically allocated blocks, use `memcpy()` instead of manually iterating through elements. This can lead to more efficient and error-resistant code. Example:

```
int *source = (int*)malloc(5 * sizeof(int));
int *destination = (int*)malloc(5 * sizeof(int));


// Properly copy memory using memcpy
memcpy(destination, source, 5 * sizeof(int));
```

Chapter 4

Pointers and Structures

4.1 Pointers to Structures

Pointers and structures are powerful features in C programming, and their combination allows for efficient handling of complex data structures. This section explores the concept of pointers to structures, demonstrating how pointers can be used to manipulate and access data within structures.

4.1.1 Understanding Structures

In C, a structure is a user-defined data type that allows bundling different types of data under a single name. The syntax for declaring a structure is as follows:

struct *structure_name*{*data_type1 member1*; *data_type2 member2*; ...};

For example:

```
struct Point { int x; int y; };
```

Here, `Point` is a structure containing two members: `x` and `y`.

4.1.2   Pointers to Structures

Pointers to structures provide a way to efficiently work with complex data by allowing direct access to the members of a structure. The general syntax for declaring a pointer to a structure is:

$$struct\_type * ptr\_name;$$

For example:

```
struct Point *ptr;
```

Here, `ptr` is a pointer to a `Point` structure.

4.1.3   Accessing Structure Members via Pointers

To access members of a structure through a pointer, the arrow operator (`->`) is used. The syntax is:

$$ptr\_name \rightarrow member\_name$$

For instance:

```
ptr->x
```

This accesses the `x` member of the structure that `ptr` points to.

4.1.4   Example: Pointers to Structures

Let's consider a practical example involving a structure representing a student:

```
#include <stdio.h>

struct Student {
    char name[50];
    int roll_number;
```

```
    float marks;
};

int main() {
    struct Student student1 = {"John Doe", 101, 85.5};

    // Pointer to a structure
    struct Student *ptr = &student1;

    // Accessing structure members via pointers
    printf("Student Name: %s\n", ptr->name);
    printf("Roll Number: %d\n", ptr->roll_number);
    printf("Marks: %.2f\n", ptr->marks);

    return 0;
}
```

In this example, a structure `Student` is defined, and a pointer `ptr` is used to access and print the members of a `Student` structure.

4.1.5 Numerical Example: Calculating Average Marks

Consider a scenario where a program needs to calculate the average marks of a group of students. A structure representing a student is defined, and a function is created to compute the average marks using an array of structures and pointers:

```
#include <stdio.h>

struct Student {
    char name[50];
    float marks;
```

```c
};


float calculateAverage(struct Student *students, int num_students) {
    float total_marks = 0;

    // Calculate total marks
    for (int i = 0; i < num_students; i++) {
        total_marks += students[i].marks;
    }

    // Calculate average
    float average = total_marks / num_students;
    return average;
}


int main() {
    // Array of structures
    struct Student class[5]
        = {{"Alice", 78.5}, {"Bob", 92.0}, {"Charlie", 85.5},
                              {"David", 90.0}, {"Eva", 88.5}};

    // Pointer to structures
    struct Student *ptr = class;

    // Calculate and print average marks
    printf("Average Marks: %.2f\n", calculateAverage(ptr, 5));

    return 0;
}
```

In this numerical example, a function `calculateAverage` takes a pointer to an array of structures and the number of students, then computes and returns the average marks.

4.1.6 Best Practices for Pointers to Structures

When working with pointers to structures, it is essential to follow best practices:

1. **Check for NULL:** Always check if a pointer to a structure is not NULL before accessing its members to avoid runtime errors.

2. **Initialize Pointers:** Initialize pointers to structures before accessing or modifying their members. Uninitialized pointers lead to undefined behavior.

3. **Use -> for Access:** Use the arrow operator (->) for accessing structure members through pointers for clarity and readability.

4. **Avoid Type Mismatch:** Ensure that the pointer type matches the type of the structure to avoid type-related issues.

5. **Document Structure Members:** Clearly document the structure members and their expected types for proper usage.

6. **Dynamic Memory Allocation:** When dealing with dynamic memory allocation for structures, remember to free allocated memory to prevent memory leaks.

7. **Avoid Dangling Pointers:** Be cautious of pointers becoming dangling pointers. Ensure that pointers point to valid memory locations.

8. **Use Meaningful Pointer Names:** Use meaningful names for pointers to improve code readability and understanding.

9. **Consistent Naming Conventions:** Adopt consistent naming conventions for structures and their members to enhance code maintainability.

10. **Error Handling:** Implement appropriate error handling mechanisms, especially when dealing with dynamic memory allocation and pointers.

11. **Review Code Periodically:** Regularly review code that involves pointers to structures to identify and address potential issues.

12. **Testing:** Perform thorough testing, including boundary testing and error scenarios, to ensure the robustness of code using pointers to structures.

By adhering to these best practices, programmers can effectively leverage pointers to structures in C, leading to code that is more readable, maintainable, and less prone to errors.

4.2   Passing Structures to Functions

Passing structures to functions is a common practice in C, allowing functions to operate on complex data structures efficiently. This section delves into the nuances of passing structures to functions, emphasizing the use of pointers for better performance.

4.2.1   Passing Structures by Value

In C, structures can be passed to functions by value. When a structure is passed by value, a copy of the entire structure is made, and the function works with this copy. While straightforward, this method may lead to inefficiency for large structures due to the overhead of copying.

```
#include <stdio.h>

struct Point {
    int x;
    int y;
};

void displayPoint(struct Point p) {
    printf("Point Coordinates: (%d, %d)\n", p.x, p.y);
}

int main() {
    struct Point origin = {0, 0};
    displayPoint(origin);
```

```
    return 0;
}
```

In the example above, the `displayPoint` function takes a `struct Point` parameter by value.

4.2.2   Passing Structures by Pointer

To avoid the overhead of copying large structures, structures are often passed to functions by pointer. Passing a pointer to a structure allows the function to work directly with the original structure, minimizing memory and runtime costs.

```c
#include <stdio.h>

struct Point {
    int x;
    int y;
};

void displayPoint(struct Point *p) {
    printf("Point Coordinates: (%d, %d)\n", p->x, p->y);
}

int main() {
    struct Point origin = {0, 0};
    displayPoint(&origin);

    return 0;
}
```

Here, the `displayPoint` function takes a pointer to a `struct Point`, providing more efficiency for large structures.

4.2.3   Passing Structures to Modify Data

Passing structures to functions is not limited to displaying data; structures can also be passed for modification. When a structure is passed to modify its data, using a pointer becomes imperative to ensure changes reflect in the original structure.

```
#include <stdio.h>

struct Rectangle {
    int length;
    int width;
};

void scaleRectangle(struct Rectangle *rect, int scaleFactor) {
    rect->length *= scaleFactor;
    rect->width *= scaleFactor;
}

int main() {
    struct Rectangle box = {5, 3};
    scaleRectangle(&box, 2);

    printf("Scaled Rectangle:
    Length=%d, Width=%d\n", box.length, box.width);

    return 0;
}
```

In this example, the scaleRectangle function modifies the dimensions of a rectangle passed by pointer.

4.2.4 Numerical Example: Computing Area of Rectangle

Consider a scenario where a program needs to compute the area of a rectangle. A structure representing a rectangle is defined, and a function is created to calculate the area using pointers:

```c
#include <stdio.h>

struct Rectangle {
    float length;
    float width;
};

float calculateArea(const struct Rectangle *rect) {
    return rect->length * rect->width;
}

int main() {
    struct Rectangle myRect = {4.5, 3.2};
    float area = calculateArea(&myRect);

    printf("Rectangle Area: %.2f square units\n", area);

    return 0;
}
```

Here, the `calculateArea` function takes a pointer to a `struct Rectangle` to compute the area, showcasing the practical use of passing structures to functions.

4.2.5   Best Practices for Passing Structures to Functions

When passing structures to functions, certain best practices enhance code clarity, maintainability, and performance:

1. **Use Pointers for Large Structures:** For large structures, prefer passing pointers to avoid the overhead of copying.

2. **Consider Passing by Const Reference:** When modification is not required, consider passing structures by const reference to emphasize read-only access.

3. **Check for NULL:** When passing pointers to structures, always check if the pointer is not NULL before dereferencing to prevent runtime errors.

4. **Document Function Contracts:** Clearly document whether a function expects a pointer to a structure or the structure itself. Include information on whether the structure may be modified.

5. **Use Meaningful Variable and Function Names:** Choose meaningful names for structure members, variables, and functions to enhance code readability.

6. **Avoid Excessive Modification:** Limit the modification of structures within functions to enhance code maintainability and prevent unintended side effects.

7. **Consistent Naming Conventions:** Adopt consistent naming conventions for structures, their members, and functions that operate on them.

8. **Test Edge Cases:** Perform thorough testing, including edge cases and scenarios involving NULL pointers, to ensure the robustness of functions.

9. **Consider Error Handling:** Implement appropriate error handling mechanisms, especially when dealing with pointers and potential memory allocation issues.

10. **Review Code Periodically:** Regularly review code that involves passing structures to functions to identify and address potential issues.

By adhering to these best practices, programmers can effectively pass structures to functions in a manner that promotes code reliability and readability.

4.3 Dynamic Allocation for Structures

Dynamic allocation is a powerful feature in C, allowing programs to manage memory dynamically during runtime. When working with structures, dynamic allocation becomes particularly useful for handling variable-sized data. This section explores the dynamic allocation of structures using pointers, providing examples and insights into best practices.

4.3.1 Dynamic Memory Allocation in C

Dynamic memory allocation in C is achieved through functions like `malloc()`, `calloc()`, `realloc()`, and `free()`. These functions enable the allocation and deallocation of memory blocks during program execution. The general syntax for dynamic allocation is:

```
type *ptr = (type*)malloc(size);
```

Here, `ptr` is a pointer to the allocated memory block, and `size` is the size of the memory block in bytes.

4.3.2 Dynamic Allocation for Structures

When dealing with structures, dynamic allocation allows the creation of structures with varying sizes, promoting flexibility in program design. The process involves allocating memory for the structure using `malloc()` or `calloc()` and then using a pointer to access and manipulate the structure's members.

```
#include <stdio.h>
#include <stdlib.h>

struct Point {
    int x;
    int y;
};
```

```c
int main() {
    // Dynamic allocation for a Point structure
    struct Point *ptr = (struct Point*)malloc(sizeof(struct Point));

    // Check if allocation is successful
    if (ptr != NULL) {
        // Accessing and modifying structure members
        ptr->x = 5;
        ptr->y = 10;

        // Displaying structure contents
        printf("Point Coordinates: (%d, %d)\n", ptr->x, ptr->y);

        // Freeing allocated memory
        free(ptr);
    } else {
        fprintf(stderr, "Memory allocation failed");
    }

    return 0;
}
```

In this example, memory is dynamically allocated for a `Point` structure, and its members are accessed using a pointer.

4.3.3   Numerical Example: Creating an Array of Structures

Dynamic allocation is especially beneficial when dealing with arrays of structures of variable sizes. Consider a scenario where a program needs to manage an array of points whose size is determined at runtime:

```c
#include <stdio.h>
#include <stdlib.h>

struct Point {
    int x;
    int y;
};

int main() {
    int numPoints;

    // Get the number of points from the user
    printf("Enter the number of points: ");
    scanf("%d", &numPoints);

    // Dynamic allocation for an array of Point structures
    struct Point *pointArray = (struct Point*)malloc(numPoints * sizeof(struct Point));

    // Check if allocation is successful
    if (pointArray != NULL) {
        // Initialize and display the array
        for (int i = 0; i < numPoints; i++) {
            pointArray[i].x = i + 1;
            pointArray[i].y = 2 * (i + 1);
            printf("Point %d: (%d, %d)\n", i + 1, pointArray[i].x, pointArray[i].y);
        }

        // Freeing allocated memory
        free(pointArray);
    } else {
        fprintf(stderr, "Memory allocation failed");
```

```
    }


    return 0;
}
```

Here, an array of `Point` structures is dynamically allocated based on user input, demonstrating the flexibility of dynamic allocation for structures.

4.3.4   Best Practices for Dynamic Allocation of Structures

When dynamically allocating structures, certain best practices ensure proper memory management and program stability:

1. **Check for NULL After Allocation:** Always check if the pointer returned by `malloc()` or `calloc()` is not `NULL` before accessing or modifying structure members.

2. **Free Allocated Memory:** After using dynamically allocated memory, free it using the `free()` function to prevent memory leaks.

3. **Initialize Pointers After Allocation:** Immediately initialize pointers after dynamic memory allocation to prevent the use of uninitialized memory.

4. **Use `sizeof` for Type-Safe Allocation:** When allocating memory, use `sizeof` with the type of the variable to ensure type safety and avoid hardcoding sizes.

5. **Document Ownership and Lifespan:** Clearly document the ownership and expected lifespan of dynamically allocated memory to avoid unintended deallocation or reference issues.

6. **Error Handling:** Implement appropriate error-handling mechanisms for cases where dynamic allocation may fail, such as when there is insufficient memory.

7. **Avoid Fragmentation with `realloc()`:** When resizing dynamically allocated memory, use `realloc()` carefully to avoid fragmentation and unnecessary resizing.

8. **Use Meaningful Variable Names:** Choose meaningful names for pointers to structures and dynamically allocated memory to enhance code readability.

9. **Test for Memory Leaks:** Regularly test programs for memory leaks using tools like Valgrind to catch issues early in the development process.

10. **Use `calloc()` for Zero Initialization:** When allocating memory that needs to be initialized to zero, prefer `calloc()` over `malloc()` for clarity and efficiency.

11. **Clear Pointers After Freeing:** After freeing dynamically allocated memory, set the pointer to `NULL` to prevent accidental use of a dangling pointer.

12. **Use `memcpy()` for Memory Copying:** When copying data between dynamically allocated blocks, use `memcpy()` for more efficient and error-resistant code.

By following these best practices, programmers can harness the full potential of dynamic allocation for structures in C, leading to code that is more robust, readable, and maintainable.

Chapter 5

Pointers and Strings

5.1 String Basics in C

Strings in C are represented as arrays of characters, terminated by a null character (')

0'). Pointers play a crucial role in manipulating and working with strings efficiently. This section explores the fundamentals of strings in C, emphasizing the use of pointers for various string operations.

5.1.1 String Declaration and Initialization

In C, a string is essentially an array of characters. The declaration of a string involves specifying the array type and size, followed by initialization with a sequence of characters. The null character marks the end of the string.

```
char str1[10] = \Hello";  // Initialized with a string literal
```

Alternatively, strings can be initialized without specifying the size, letting the compiler determine the size based on the length of the string literal.

```
char str2[] = \World";  // Compiler determines size
```

73

5.1.2   String Length Calculation

To calculate the length of a string in C, one can use the `strlen()` function provided by the `string.h` library. This function iterates through the characters of the string until it encounters the null character, returning the number of characters before the null character.

```
int length = strlen(str1);  // Gets the length of str1
```

5.1.3   String Concatenation

Concatenating two strings in C can be done using the `strcat()` function. This function appends the characters of the source string to the destination string, and it assumes that the destination string has enough space to accommodate the result.

```
#include <stdio.h>
#include <string.h>

int main() {
    char str1[20] = "Hello";
    char str2[] = ", World!";

    strcat(str1, str2); // Concatenates str2 to str1

    printf("Concatenated String: %s\n", str1);

    return 0;
}
```

Here, `strcat()` is used to concatenate `str2` to `str1`, resulting in a string that contains both greetings.

5.1.4 String Copying

Copying strings in C is achieved using the `strcpy()` function. This function copies the characters of the source string to the destination string, overwriting the original content of the destination. As with concatenation, it assumes that the destination has sufficient space.

```c
#include <stdio.h>
#include <string.h>

int main() {
    char source[] = "Copy me!";
    char destination[20];

    strcpy(destination, source); // Copies source to destination

    printf("Copied String: %s\n", destination);

    return 0;
}
```

In this example, `strcpy()` is used to copy the contents of `source` to `destination`.

5.1.5 String Comparison

Comparing strings in C can be done using the `strcmp()` function. This function returns an integer value that indicates the relationship between the strings. If the result is zero, the strings are equal. A positive value indicates that the first differing character has a greater ASCII value in the first string, while a negative value indicates the opposite.

```c
#include <stdio.h>
#include <string.h>
```

```c
int main() {
    char str1[] = "Apple";
    char str2[] = "Banana";

    int result = strcmp(str1, str2);

    if (result == 0) {
        printf("The strings are equal.\n");
    } else if (result < 0) {
        printf("%s comes before %s.\n", str1, str2);
    } else {
        printf("%s comes after %s.\n", str1, str2);
    }

    return 0;
}
```

Here, `strcmp()` is used to compare `str1` and `str2`, providing information about their relationship.

5.1.6   Numerical Example: Palindrome Checking

Let's consider a practical example where a program checks if a given string is a palindrome. A palindrome is a word, phrase, or sequence of characters that reads the same forward and backward.

```c
#include <stdio.h>
#include <string.h>

int isPalindrome(const char *str) {
    int length = strlen(str);
```

```c
    for (int i = 0; i < length / 2; i++) {
        if (str[i] != str[length - 1 - i]) {
            return 0; // Not a palindrome
        }
    }


    return 1; // Palindrome
}


int main() {
    char input[50];

    printf("Enter a string: ");
    scanf("%s", input);

    if (isPalindrome(input)) {
        printf("The string is a palindrome.\n");
    } else {
        printf("The string is not a palindrome.\n");
    }

    return 0;
}
```

In this example, the program prompts the user for a string and uses the isPalindrome() function to determine if it is a palindrome.

5.1.7 Best Practices for String Handling in C

Effective string handling in C requires adherence to best practices to ensure code reliability and security:

1. **Buffer Size Consideration:** Always ensure that destination buffers

have sufficient size to accommodate the result of string operations to prevent buffer overflows.

2. **Use `sizeof` for Buffer Sizes:** When allocating or declaring buffers, use `sizeof` to specify the size based on the type to avoid hardcoding.

3. **Check Return Values:** Functions like `strcpy()`, `strcat()`, and `malloc()` may fail, and their return values should be checked for `NULL` to handle errors gracefully.

4. **Use `strncpy()` for Bounded Copy:** Instead of `strcpy()`, consider using `strncpy()` for bounded string copying to prevent buffer overflows.

5. **Use `snprintf()` for Safer Formatting:** When formatting strings, prefer `snprintf()` over `sprintf()` to prevent buffer overflows by specifying the maximum number of characters to write.

6. **Avoid Direct Array Modification:** Avoid direct modification of individual characters in a string, especially when null termination needs to be maintained.

7. **Use `const` for Read-Only Strings:** Use the `const` qualifier for read-only strings to indicate that the string should not be modified.

8. **Understand Null Termination:** Always ensure that strings are properly null-terminated, and be aware that certain functions may not work correctly if this convention is not followed.

9. **Handle User Input Safely:** When accepting user input, use functions like `fgets()` instead of `scanf()` to prevent buffer overflows and handle newline characters.

10. **Secure Password Handling:** Avoid storing passwords as plain text in memory and use secure functions like `getpass()` when handling sensitive information.

11. **Regularly Check for Memory Leaks:** When dynamically allocating memory for strings, regularly check for memory leaks using tools like Valgrind to ensure efficient memory management.

12. **Use `strncat()` for Bounded Concatenation:** Instead of `strcat()`, consider using `strncat()` for safer bounded string concatenation.

By adhering to these best practices, developers can create robust and secure C programs that effectively handle strings using pointers.

5.2 Pointers and String Manipulation

Pointers play a pivotal role in C when it comes to string manipulation. Understanding how pointers can be utilized for efficient string operations is essential for every C programmer. This section delves into various string manipulation techniques using pointers, providing real working examples and insights into the underlying mechanisms.

5.2.1 Accessing Individual Characters

In C, strings are essentially arrays of characters terminated by a null character ['\0']. Pointers can be used to iterate through the characters of a string and perform operations on each character.

```c
char *str = "Hello";
char *ptr = str;
while (*ptr != '\0') {
    printf("%c-", *ptr);
    ptr++;
}
```

In this example, a pointer `ptr` is used to access and print each character of the string "Hello" until the null character is encountered.

5.2.2 String Reversal

Reversing a string is a common string manipulation task. Pointers can be employed to achieve this efficiently.

```c
#include <stdio.h>
```

```c
void reverseString(char *str) {
    char *start = str;
    char *end = str;

    // Move end to the end of the string
    while (*end != '\0') {
        end++;
    }
    end--;

    // Reverse the string
    while (start < end) {
        // Swap characters
        char temp = *start;
        *start = *end;
        *end = temp;

        // Move pointers
        start++;
        end--;
    }
}

int main() {
    char myString[] = "World";
    reverseString(myString);

    printf("Reversed String: %s\n", myString);

    return 0;
}
```

This code defines a function `reverseString` that reverses the input string using pointers. The reversed string is then printed in the `main()` function.

5.2.3 String Tokenization

String tokenization involves breaking a string into tokens (substrings) based on a delimiter. Pointers simplify the process of traversing and extracting tokens from a string.

```c
#include <stdio.h>
#include <string.h>

void tokenizeString(char *str, const char *delimiter) {
    char *token = strtok(str, delimiter);

    while (token != NULL) {
        printf("Token: %s\n", token);
        token = strtok(NULL, delimiter);
    }
}


int main() {
    char sentence[] = "This is a sample sentence.";
    char delimiter[] = " ";

    tokenizeString(sentence, delimiter);

    return 0;
}
```

In this example, the function `tokenizeString` uses pointers and the `strtok()` function to tokenize the input sentence based on spaces.

5.2.4 String Concatenation using Pointers

Concatenating strings using pointers involves careful pointer arithmetic to navigate to the end of the first string and then copy the characters of the second string.

```c
#include <stdio.h>

void concatenateStrings(char *str1, const char *str2) {
    // Move to the end of str1
    while (*str1 != '\0') {
        str1++;
    }

    // Copy characters from str2 to str1
    while (*str2 != '\0') {
        *str1 = *str2;
        str1++;
        str2++;
    }

    // Null-terminate the result
    *str1 = '\0';
}

int main() {
    char string1[20] = "Hello, ";
    const char *string2 = "World!";

    concatenateStrings(string1, string2);

    printf("Concatenated String: %s\n", string1);
```

```
    return 0;
}
```

This code defines a function `concatenateStrings` that concatenates two strings using pointers and then prints the result in the `main()` function.

5.2.5 Numerical Example: Searching for Substrings

Consider a scenario where a program needs to check if a substring exists within a given string. Pointers can be employed to efficiently search for substrings.

```
#include <stdio.h>

int containsSubstring(const char *str, const char *sub) {
    while (*str != '\0') {
        const char *strPtr = str;
        const char *subPtr = sub;

        // Check if the substring is present at the current position
        while (*subPtr != '\0' && *strPtr == *subPtr) {
            strPtr++;
            subPtr++;
        }

        // If the substring is found, return 1
        if (*subPtr == '\0') {
            return 1;
        }

        // Move to the next position in the string
        str++;
```

```
    }


    // Substring not found
    return 0;
}


int main() {
    const char *mainString = "Programming is fun!";
    const char *substring = "is";


    if (containsSubstring(mainString, substring)) {
        printf("The substring is present.\n");
    } else {
        printf("The substring is not present.\n");
    }


    return 0;
}
```

In this example, the function `containsSubstring` uses pointers to efficiently search for a substring within a given string.

5.2.6   Best Practices for Pointers and String Manipulation

Efficient and secure string manipulation with pointers involves following best practices:

1. **Null Termination:** Ensure that strings are null-terminated to prevent undefined behavior.

2. **Boundary Checking:** Exercise caution to avoid buffer overflows by checking string boundaries during manipulation.

3. **Use `const` Correctly:** Utilize `const` appropriately for read-only strings to prevent accidental modifications.

4. **Error Handling:** Check return values of string manipulation functions like `strtok()` and `strncpy()` for potential errors.

5. **Avoid Dangling Pointers:** Be mindful of pointer lifetimes and avoid using pointers that point to deallocated memory.

6. **Dynamic Memory Allocation:** When manipulating strings dynamically, allocate sufficient memory and free it appropriately to avoid memory leaks.

7. **Understand Pointer Arithmetic:** Gain a deep understanding of pointer arithmetic, especially when manipulating strings character by character.

8. **Use Library Functions Wisely:** Leverage standard library functions like `strncpy()`, `strncat()`, and `strstr()` for safer string manipulation.

9. **String Length Calculation:** Utilize `strlen()` for calculating string lengths and avoid manual counting to improve code readability.

10. **Pointer Initialization:** Initialize pointers immediately after declaration to prevent the use of uninitialized pointers.

11. **Clear Pointers After Freeing:** Set pointers to `NULL` after freeing dynamic memory to avoid dangling pointers.

12. **Documentation:** Clearly document the assumptions and constraints of functions that manipulate strings using pointers.

By incorporating these best practices, programmers can enhance the reliability, efficiency, and security of string manipulation in C using pointers.

5.3 String Functions and Pointers

String functions in C, such as those provided by the `string.h` library, play a crucial role in string manipulation. When combined with pointers, these functions become powerful tools for working with strings efficiently. This section explores various string functions and demonstrates how they can be effectively used with pointers through real working examples.

5.3.1   Introduction to String Functions

The `string.h` library in C includes several functions for manipulating strings. These functions are particularly useful when dealing with tasks such as copying, concatenating, comparing, and tokenizing strings. Pointers enhance the versatility of these functions, allowing for dynamic and efficient string manipulation.

5.3.2   Copying Strings with `strcpy()`

The `strcpy()` function is used to copy one string to another. It takes two arguments: the destination string and the source string. Pointers can be employed to manipulate the strings efficiently.

```c
char source[] = "Hello, World!";
char destination[20];
char *sourcePtr = source;
char *destPtr = destination;
while (*sourcePtr != '\0') {
    *destPtr = *sourcePtr;
    sourcePtr++;
    destPtr++;
}
*destPtr = '\0';
```

In this example, `source` is copied to `destination` using pointers to iterate through each character and null-terminate the destination.

5.3.3   Concatenating Strings with `strcat()`

The `strcat()` function is employed to concatenate one string to the end of another. It appends the characters of the source string to the destination string.

```c
#include <stdio.h>
#include <string.h>
```

```
int main() {
    char str1[20] = "Hello, ";
    char str2[] = "World!";

    strcat(str1, str2); // Concatenates str2 to str1

    printf("Concatenated String: %s\n", str1);

    return 0;
}
```

Here, `strcat()` is used to concatenate `str2` to `str1`, resulting in a string that contains both greetings.

5.3.4 Comparing Strings with `strcmp()`

The `strcmp()` function is used to compare two strings. It returns an integer value indicating their relationship. A zero value means the strings are equal.

```
#include <stdio.h>
#include <string.h>

int main() {
    char str1[] = "Apple";
    char str2[] = "Banana";

    int result = strcmp(str1, str2);

    if (result == 0) {
        printf("The strings are equal.\n");
    } else if (result < 0) {
        printf("%s comes before %s.\n", str1, str2);
```

```
    } else {
        printf("%s comes after %s.\n", str1, str2);
    }


    return 0;
}
```

In this example, strcmp() is used to compare str1 and str2, providing information about their relationship.

5.3.5   Finding Substrings with strstr()

The strstr() function is employed to find the first occurrence of a substring within a string. It returns a pointer to the located substring or NULL if the substring is not found.

```
#include <stdio.h>
#include <string.h>

int main() {
    char mainStr[] = "This is a sample sentence.";
    char subStr[] = "sample";

    char *result = strstr(mainStr, subStr);

    if (result != NULL) {
        printf("Substring found at position: %ld\n", result - mainStr);
    } else {
        printf("Substring not found.\n");
    }


    return 0;
}
```

In this example, `strstr()` is used to find the position of the substring `sample` in the main string.

5.3.6   Tokenizing Strings with `strtok()`

The `strtok()` function is employed to tokenize a string based on a specified delimiter. It returns a pointer to the next token.

```c
#include <stdio.h>
#include <string.h>

int main() {
    char sentence[] = "This is a sample sentence.";
    char *delimiter = " ";

    char *token = strtok(sentence, delimiter);

    while (token != NULL) {
        printf("Token: %s\n", token);
        token = strtok(NULL, delimiter);
    }

    return 0;
}
```

Here, `strtok()` is used to tokenize the sentence based on spaces, and each token is printed.

5.3.7   Numerical Example: Reversing a String

Consider a scenario where a program needs to reverse a given string. Pointers can be employed for efficient string reversal.

```c
#include <stdio.h>
```

```c
#include <string.h>

void reverseString(char *str) {
    char *start = str;
    char *end = str + strlen(str) - 1;

    while (start < end) {
        char temp = *start;
        *start = *end;
        *end = temp;

        start++;
        end--;
    }
}

int main() {
    char myString[] = "Reverse This";
    reverseString(myString);

    printf("Reversed String: %s\n", myString);

    return 0;
}
```

In this example, the function `reverseString()` uses pointers to reverse the input string `myString`.

5.3.8   Best Practices for String Functions and Pointers

Efficient use of string functions with pointers involves adhering to best practices:

1. **Null Termination:** Ensure that strings are null-terminated to prevent

undefined behavior.

2. **Buffer Size Consideration:** Be cautious about buffer sizes to prevent buffer overflows.

3. **Pointer Initialization:** Initialize pointers immediately after declaration to prevent the use of uninitialized pointers.

4. **Error Handling:** Check return values of string functions for potential errors.

5. **Boundary Checking:** Exercise caution to avoid buffer overflows by checking string boundaries during manipulation.

6. **Use `const` Correctly:** Utilize `const` appropriately for read-only strings to prevent accidental modifications.

7. **Dynamic Memory Allocation:** When manipulating strings dynamically, allocate sufficient memory and free it appropriately to avoid memory leaks.

8. **Understand Pointer Arithmetic:** Gain a deep understanding of pointer arithmetic, especially when manipulating strings character by character.

9. **Use Library Functions Wisely:** Leverage standard library functions for safer string manipulation.

10. **Documentation:** Clearly document the assumptions and constraints of functions that manipulate strings using pointers.

By incorporating these best practices, programmers can enhance the reliability, efficiency, and security of string manipulation in C using pointers.

5.4 Common String Operations

String operations in C are fundamental tasks that involve manipulating strings in various ways. Pointers play a crucial role in performing these operations efficiently. This section explores common string operations, delving into formulas, real working examples, and numerical examples to provide a comprehensive understanding.

5.4.1   String Length Calculation

The length of a string is the number of characters in it until the null terminator is encountered. The `strlen()` function is commonly used for this purpose. The formula for calculating string length is:

$$\texttt{length} = \texttt{strlen}(str)$$

Here, `str` is the input string, and `length` is the calculated length.

```
#include <stdio.h>
#include <string.h>

int main() {
    char myString[] = "Hello, World!";
    size_t length = strlen(myString);

    printf("Length of the string: %zu\n", length);

    return 0;
}
```

In this example, the length of the string "Hello, World!" is calculated using `strlen()`.

5.4.2   String Copying

Copying one string to another is a common operation, and the `strcpy()` function is often used. The formula for string copying is:

$$\texttt{strcpy}(destination, source)$$

Here, `destination` is the destination string, and `source` is the source string.

```
#include <stdio.h>
```

```
#include <string.h>

int main() {
    char source[] = "Copy this string.";
    char destination[20];

    strcpy(destination, source);

    printf("Copied String: %s\n", destination);

    return 0;
}
```

In this example, the source string is copied to the destination string using strcpy().

5.4.3   String Concatenation

Concatenating strings involves combining two strings into one. The strcat()
function is commonly used for this operation. The formula for string concatenation is:

$$\text{strcat}(str1, str2)$$

Here, str1 is the destination string, and str2 is the string to be appended.

```
#include <stdio.h>
#include <string.h>

int main() {
    char str1[20] = "Hello, ";
    char str2[] = "World!";
```

```
    strcat(str1, str2);

    printf("Concatenated String: %s\n", str1);

    return 0;
}
```

In this example, str2 is concatenated to str1 using strcat().

5.4.4   String Comparison

Comparing strings is a fundamental operation, and the strcmp() function is commonly used. The formula for string comparison is:

$$result = \text{strcmp}(str1, str2)$$

Here, str1 and str2 are the strings being compared, and result is the comparison result.

```
#include <stdio.h>
#include <string.h>

int main() {
    char str1[] = "Apple";
    char str2[] = "Banana";

    int result = strcmp(str1, str2);

    if (result == 0) {
        printf("The strings are equal.\n");
    } else {
        printf("The strings are not equal.\n");
    }
```

```
    return 0;
}
```

In this example, `strcmp()` is used to compare `str1` and `str2`.

5.4.5 String Searching

Searching for a substring within a string is a common task. The `strstr()` function is used for this operation. The formula for string searching is:

$$result = \mathtt{strstr}(mainStr, subStr)$$

Here, `mainStr` is the main string, `subStr` is the substring being searched, and `result` is the pointer to the first occurrence of the substring.

```c
#include <stdio.h>
#include <string.h>

int main() {
    char mainStr[] = "This is a sample sentence.";
    char subStr[] = "sample";

    char *result = strstr(mainStr, subStr);

    if (result != NULL) {
        printf("Substring found at position: %ld\n", result - mainStr);
    } else {
        printf("Substring not found.\n");
    }

    return 0;
}
```

In this example, `strstr()` is used to find the position of the substring `sample` in the main string.

5.4.6   Numerical Example: Reversing a String

Reversing a string is a classic string manipulation task. The formula for string reversal involves swapping characters from the start and end until they meet at the center:

$$reverseString(str) = str[\texttt{length} - i] \leftrightarrow str[i]$$

Here, `str` is the input string, `length` is the length of the string, and `i` is the current iteration index.

```c
#include <stdio.h>
#include <string.h>

void reverseString(char *str) {
    size_t length = strlen(str);
    for (size_t i = 0; i < length / 2; i++) {
        char temp = str[i];
        str[i] = str[length - i - 1];
        str[length - i - 1] = temp;
    }
}

int main() {
    char myString[] = "Reverse This";
    reverseString(myString);

    printf("Reversed String: %s\n", myString);

    return 0;
```

```
}
```

In this example, the function `reverseString()` reverses the input string `myString`.

5.4.7 Best Practices for Common String Operations

Efficient use of common string operations involves following best practices:

1. **Null Termination:** Ensure that strings are null-terminated to prevent undefined behavior.

2. **Buffer Size Consideration:** Be cautious about buffer sizes to prevent buffer overflows.

3. **Pointer Initialization:** Initialize pointers immediately after declaration to prevent the use of uninitialized pointers.

4. **Error Handling:** Check return values of string functions for potential errors.

5. **Boundary Checking:** Exercise caution to avoid buffer overflows by checking string boundaries during manipulation.

6. **Use `const` Correctly:** Utilize `const` appropriately for read-only strings to prevent accidental modifications.

7. **Dynamic Memory Allocation:** When manipulating strings dynamically, allocate sufficient memory and free it appropriately to avoid memory leaks.

8. **Understand Pointer Arithmetic:** Gain a deep understanding of pointer arithmetic, especially when manipulating strings character by character.

9. **Use Library Functions Wisely:** Leverage standard library functions for safer string manipulation.

10. **Documentation:** Clearly document the assumptions and constraints of functions that manipulate strings using pointers.

By incorporating these best practices, programmers can enhance the reliability, efficiency, and security of common string operations in C using pointers.

Chapter 6

Advanced Pointer Topics

6.1 Pointers to Pointers

Pointers to pointers, also known as double pointers, are a powerful concept in C programming. They provide a way to manipulate pointers indirectly and are commonly used in scenarios where dynamic memory allocation and data manipulation are involved.

6.1.1 Overview of Pointers to Pointers

A pointer to a pointer is declared using the '**' syntax. It is used to store the address of another pointer. The formula for declaring a pointer to a pointer is:

```
type **ptr_to_ptr;
```

Here, **type** represents the data type of the underlying variable.

```c
#include <stdio.h>

int main() {
    int value = 42;
    int *ptr_to_value = &value;
```

```
    int **ptr_to_ptr = &ptr_to_value;

    printf("Value: %d\n", **ptr_to_ptr);

    return 0;
}
```

In this example, a pointer to a pointer is used to indirectly access the value stored in an integer variable.

6.1.2   Dynamic Memory Allocation with Pointers to Pointers

Pointers to pointers are particularly useful when dealing with dynamic memory allocation, as they allow for the creation of dynamic arrays and matrices.

```
#include <stdio.h>
#include <stdlib.h>

int main() {
    int rows = 3, cols = 4;

    // Allocate memory for a 2D array
    int **matrix = (int **)malloc(rows * sizeof(int *));
    for (int i = 0; i < rows; i++) {
        matrix[i] = (int *)malloc(cols * sizeof(int));
    }

    // Initialize and access elements
    for (int i = 0; i < rows; i++) {
        for (int j = 0; j < cols; j++) {
            matrix[i][j] = i * cols + j;
```

```
        printf("%d ", matrix[i][j]);
    }
    printf("\n");
}


// Free allocated memory
for (int i = 0; i < rows; i++) {
    free(matrix[i]);
}
free(matrix);


return 0;
}
```

This example demonstrates the dynamic allocation of a 2D array using pointers to pointers.

6.1.3 Function Parameters with Pointers to Pointers

Passing pointers to pointers as function parameters allows functions to modify the value of the original pointer, providing a way to return multiple values.

```
#include <stdio.h>


void modifyValue(int **ptr) {
    **ptr = 99;
}


int main() {
    int value = 42;
    int *ptr_to_value = &value;
```

```
    printf("Original Value: %d\n", *ptr_to_value);


    modifyValue(&ptr_to_value);


    printf("Modified Value: %d\n", *ptr_to_value);


    return 0;
}
```

In this example, the function 'modifyValue' modifies the value pointed to by the pointer to a pointer.

6.1.4   Pointers to Pointers and Strings

Pointers to pointers are commonly used in string manipulation scenarios, especially when dealing with dynamic memory allocation for strings.

```
#include <stdio.h>
#include <stdlib.h>


void allocateAndModifyString(char **str) {
    *str = (char *)malloc(20 * sizeof(char));
    sprintf(*str, "Dynamic String");
}


int main() {
    char *myString;


    allocateAndModifyString(&myString);


    printf("Dynamic String: %s\n", myString);
```

```
    free(myString);


    return 0;
}
```

In this example, a pointer to a pointer is used to dynamically allocate and modify a string.

6.1.5   Error Handling with Pointers to Pointers

Proper error handling is crucial when dealing with dynamic memory allocation. Pointers to pointers play a significant role in handling errors, ensuring that memory is released even in case of failures.

```
#include <stdio.h>
#include <stdlib.h>


int allocateMemory(int ***ptr) {
    *ptr = (int **)malloc(sizeof(int *));
    if (*ptr == NULL) {
        return 0; // Allocation failed
    }


    **ptr = (int *)malloc(sizeof(int));
    if (**ptr == NULL) {
        free(*ptr);
        return 0; // Allocation failed
    }


    return 1; // Allocation successful
}
```

```c
int main() {
    int **dynamicValue;

    if (allocateMemory(&dynamicValue)) {
        **dynamicValue = 123;
        printf("Dynamic Value: %d\n", **dynamicValue);

        // Free allocated memory
        free(*dynamicValue);
        free(dynamicValue);
    } else {
        printf("Memory allocation failed.\n");
    }

    return 0;
}
```

This example demonstrates error handling in dynamic memory allocation using pointers to pointers.

6.1.6   Numerical Example: Matrix Operations

Pointers to pointers are commonly employed in matrix operations, such as matrix transposition.

```c
#include <stdio.h>
#include <stdlib.h>

void transposeMatrix(int **matrix, int rows, int cols) {
    int **transposed = (int **)malloc(cols * sizeof(int *));
    for (int i = 0; i < cols; i++) {
        transposed[i] = (int *)malloc(rows * sizeof(int));
```

```c
    }

    for (int i = 0; i < rows; i++) {
        for (int j = 0; j < cols; j++) {
            transposed[j][i] = matrix[i][j];
        }
    }

    // Print the transposed matrix
    for (int i = 0; i < cols; i++) {
        for (int j = 0; j < rows; j++) {
            printf("%d ", transposed[i][j]);
        }
        printf("\n");
    }

    // Free allocated memory
    for (int i = 0; i < cols; i++) {
        free(transposed[i]);
    }
    free(transposed);
}

int main() {
    int rows = 3, cols = 4;

    int **original = (int **)malloc(rows * sizeof(int *));
    for (int i = 0; i < rows; i++) {
        original[i] = (int *)malloc(cols * sizeof(int));
        for (int j = 0; j < cols; j++) {
            original[i][j] = i * cols + j + 1;
```

```
        }
    }

    printf("Original Matrix:\n");
    for (int i = 0; i < rows; i++) {
        for (int j = 0; j < cols; j++) {
            printf("%d ", original[i][j]);
        }
        printf("\n");
    }

    printf("\nTransposed Matrix:\n");
    transposeMatrix(original, rows, cols);

    // Free allocated memory
    for (int i = 0; i < rows; i++) {
        free(original[i]);
    }
    free(original);

    return 0;
}
```

In this example, the function 'transposeMatrix' transposes a matrix using pointers to pointers.

6.1.7   Best Practices and Considerations

When working with pointers to pointers, consider the following best practices:

1. **Clear Memory Allocation:** Always free allocated memory to avoid memory leaks. 2. **Error Handling:** Implement robust error handling to manage failures in dynamic memory allocation. 3. **Documentation:** Clearly

document the use of pointers to pointers in your code for better understanding.

By understanding and applying these concepts, programmers can harness the power of pointers to pointers for advanced memory management and data manipulation in C.

6.2 Void Pointers

Void pointers, often denoted as `void*`, are a versatile feature in C that allows the storage of addresses of objects of any data type. They are used in scenarios where the data type of a pointer is unknown or when a function needs to work with different data types through a single interface.

6.2.1 Overview of Void Pointers

A void pointer is declared using the `void*` syntax. It is a generic pointer that can point to objects of any data type. The formula for declaring a void pointer is:

```
void *ptr;
```

Here, `ptr` is the name of the void pointer.

```
#include <stdio.h>

int main() {
    int intValue = 42;
    float floatValue = 3.14;
    char charValue = 'A';

    void *genericPtr;

    // Assigning addresses of different data types to the void pointer
    genericPtr = &intValue;
```

```
    printf("Integer Value: %d\n", *(int *)genericPtr);


    genericPtr = &floatValue;
    printf("Float Value: %.2f\n", *(float *)genericPtr);


    genericPtr = &charValue;
    printf("Character Value: %c\n", *(char *)genericPtr);


    return 0;
}
```

In this example, a void pointer is used to point to variables of different data types.

6.2.2   Dynamic Memory Allocation with Void Pointers

Void pointers are commonly used in dynamic memory allocation scenarios where the data type may vary. Functions like `malloc()` return void pointers, allowing flexibility in handling different data types.

```
#include <stdio.h>
#include <stdlib.h>


int main() {
    int *intPtr;
    float *floatPtr;

    void *genericPtr;

    // Allocate memory for an integer
    intPtr = (int *)malloc(sizeof(int));
    *intPtr = 123;
```

```
    // Allocate memory for a float
    floatPtr = (float *)malloc(sizeof(float));
    *floatPtr = 3.14;

    // Use a void pointer to access and print values
    genericPtr = intPtr;
    printf("Integer Value: %d\n", *(int *)genericPtr);

    genericPtr = floatPtr;
    printf("Float Value: %.2f\n", *(float *)genericPtr);

    // Free allocated memory
    free(intPtr);
    free(floatPtr);

    return 0;
}
```

This example demonstrates dynamic memory allocation using void pointers for different data types.

6.2.3 Function Parameters with Void Pointers

Void pointers are often used in function parameters to create functions that can accept arguments of various data types.

```
#include <stdio.h>

void printValue(void *ptr, char type) {
    switch (type) {
        case 'i':
```

```c
            printf("Integer Value: %d\n", *(int *)ptr);
            break;
        case 'f':
            printf("Float Value: %.2f\n", *(float *)ptr);
            break;
        case 'c':
            printf("Character Value: %c\n", *(char *)ptr);
            break;
        default:
            printf("Unsupported data type\n");
    }
}


int main() {
    int intValue = 42;
    float floatValue = 3.14;
    char charValue = 'A';

    // Using void pointers in function parameters
    printValue(&intValue, 'i');
    printValue(&floatValue, 'f');
    printValue(&charValue, 'c');

    return 0;
}
```

In this example, the function `printValue()` accepts a void pointer and a character indicating the data type.

6.2.4 Numerical Example: Generic Linked List

A practical application of void pointers is in the implementation of a generic linked list. A void pointer can be used to store the data in each node, allowing the creation of a linked list that can hold any data type.

```c
#include <stdio.h>
#include <stdlib.h>


struct Node {
    void *data;
    struct Node *next;
};


void printIntList(struct Node *head) {
    struct Node *current = head;
    while (current != NULL) {
        printf("%d ", *(int *)current->data);
        current = current->next;
    }
    printf("\n");
}


void printFloatList(struct Node *head) {
    struct Node *current = head;
    while (current != NULL) {
        printf("%.2f ", *(float *)current->data);
        current = current->next;
    }
    printf("\n");
}
```

```c
int main() {
    struct Node *headInt = NULL;
    struct Node *headFloat = NULL;

    // Add integers to the linked list
    for (int i = 1; i <= 5; i++) {
        struct Node *newNode = (struct Node *)malloc(sizeof(struct Node));
        newNode->data = (int *)malloc(sizeof(int));
        *(int *)newNode->data = i * 10;
        newNode->next = headInt;
        headInt = newNode;
    }

    // Add floats to the linked list
    for (int i = 1; i <= 5; i++) {
        struct Node *newNode = (struct Node *)malloc(sizeof(struct Node));
        newNode->data = (float *)malloc(sizeof(float));
        *(float *)newNode->data = i * 3.14;
        newNode->next = headFloat;
        headFloat = newNode;
    }

    // Print linked lists
    printf("Integer Linked List: ");
    printIntList(headInt);

    printf("Float Linked List: ");
    printFloatList(headFloat);

    // Free allocated memory
    struct Node *currentInt = headInt;
```

```c
    while (currentInt != NULL) {
        struct Node *temp = currentInt;
        currentInt = currentInt->next;
        free(temp->data);
        free(temp);
    }


    struct Node *currentFloat = headFloat;
    while (currentFloat != NULL) {
        struct Node *temp = currentFloat;
        currentFloat = currentFloat->next;
        free(temp->data);
        free(temp);
    }


    return 0;
}
```

In this example, a generic linked list is implemented using void pointers to store data of different data types in each node.

6.2.5 Best Practices and Considerations

When working with void pointers, consider the following best practices:

1. **Type Safety:** Exercise caution when using void pointers to ensure type safety. 2. **Documentation:** Clearly document the data type expected when using void pointers in a particular context. 3. **Memory Management:** Properly manage memory, especially when using void pointers in dynamic memory allocation scenarios.

By understanding and applying these concepts, programmers can leverage the flexibility of void pointers for handling different data types in a generic manner.

6.3   Function Pointers

Function pointers in C provide a powerful mechanism to treat functions as first-class citizens. They allow functions to be assigned to variables, passed as arguments to other functions, and returned from functions. Understanding function pointers is crucial for implementing advanced programming constructs and improving code modularity.

6.3.1   Overview of Function Pointers

A function pointer is a variable that stores the address of a function. It is declared using the following syntax:

```
return_type (*pointer_name)(parameter_types);
```

Here, `return_type` is the return type of the function, `pointer_name` is the name of the function pointer, and `parameter_types` are the types of parameters the function takes.

```c
#include <stdio.h>

// Example function
int add(int a, int b) {
    return a + b;
}

int main() {
    // Declaration of a function pointer
    int (*addPtr)(int, int);

    // Assignment of the function to the pointer
    addPtr = &add;
```

```
    // Calling the function through the pointer
    int result = addPtr(3, 4);

    printf("Result: %d\n", result);

    return 0;
}
```

In this example, a function pointer `addPtr` is declared, assigned the address of the `add` function, and then used to call the function.

6.3.2 Function Pointers as Arguments

Function pointers can be passed as arguments to other functions, providing a way to implement generic algorithms or callbacks.

```
#include <stdio.h>

// Function that applies a function pointer to two integers
int applyOperation(int a, int b, int (*operation)(int, int)) {
    return operation(a, b);
}

// Example functions
int add(int a, int b) {
    return a + b;
}

int multiply(int a, int b) {
    return a * b;
}
```

```c
int main() {
    int resultAdd = applyOperation(3, 4, add);
    int resultMultiply = applyOperation(3, 4, multiply);

    printf("Result of addition: %d\n", resultAdd);
    printf("Result of multiplication: %d\n", resultMultiply);

    return 0;
}
```

In this example, the `applyOperation` function takes two integers and a function pointer as arguments, allowing different operations to be applied.

6.3.3   Function Pointers in Arrays

Function pointers can be used in arrays, providing a concise way to create arrays of functions.

```c
#include <stdio.h>

// Example functions
int add(int a, int b) {
    return a + b;
}

int subtract(int a, int b) {
    return a - b;
}

int multiply(int a, int b) {
    return a * b;
}
```

```
int main() {
    // Array of function pointers
    int (*operations[3])(int, int) = {add, subtract, multiply};

    // Using the function pointers from the array
    for (int i = 0; i < 3; i++) {
        int result = operations[i](5, 3);
        printf("Result of operation %d: %d\n", i + 1, result);
    }

    return 0;
}
```

Here, an array of function pointers is used to store different operations, and each function pointer is invoked in a loop.

6.3.4   Function Pointers and Callbacks

One of the powerful applications of function pointers is in implementing callbacks. Callback functions are functions that are passed as arguments to other functions, allowing customization of behavior.

```
#include <stdio.h>

// Callback function type
typedef int (*OperationCallback)(int, int);

// Function that performs an operation and calls a callback
int performOperation(int a, int b, OperationCallback callback) {
    int result = callback(a, b);
    printf("Operation Result: %d\n", result);
```

```
    return result;
}


// Example callback functions
int add(int a, int b) {
    return a + b;
}


int multiply(int a, int b) {
    return a * b;
}


int main() {
    performOperation(3, 4, add);
    performOperation(3, 4, multiply);

    return 0;
}
```

In this example, the `performOperation` function takes two integers and a callback function, allowing different operations to be performed with customized behavior.

6.3.5   Numerical Example: Sorting with Function Pointers

A common application of function pointers is in implementing sorting algorithms that allow custom comparison functions.

```
#include <stdio.h>
#include <stdlib.h>


// Comparison function type
```

```c
typedef int (*ComparisonCallback)(const void *, const void *);


// Function to perform sorting
void customSort(int arr[], size_t size, ComparisonCallback compare) {
    qsort(arr, size, sizeof(int), compare);
}


// Example comparison functions
int ascendingOrder(const void *a, const void *b) {
    return (*(int *)a - *(int *)b);
}


int descendingOrder(const void *a, const void *b) {
    return (*(int *)b - *(int *)a);
}


int main() {
    int numbers[] = {5, 2, 8, 1, 7};
    size_t size = sizeof(numbers) / sizeof(numbers[0]);

    // Sorting in ascending order
    customSort(numbers, size, ascendingOrder);

    printf("Sorted in ascending order: ");
    for (size_t i = 0; i < size; i++) {
        printf("%d ", numbers[i]);
    }
    printf("\n");

    // Sorting in descending order
    customSort(numbers, size, descendingOrder);
```

```
printf("Sorted in descending order: ");
for (size_t i = 0; i < size; i++) {
    printf("%d ", numbers[i]);
}
printf("\n");


return 0;
}
```

In this example, the `customSort` function uses a function pointer for custom comparison during sorting.

6.3.6 Best Practices and Considerations

When working with function pointers, consider the following best practices:

1. **Type Matching:** Ensure that the function pointer type matches the function it points to. 2. **Documentation:** Clearly document the expected behavior of callback functions. 3. **Error Handling:** Implement robust error handling for cases where function pointers might be NULL or improperly used.

By mastering function pointers, programmers can enhance code flexibility and create more modular and reusable software components.

6.4 Pointers and Multidimensional Arrays

Multidimensional arrays in C are essentially arrays of arrays. Understanding how pointers interact with multidimensional arrays is crucial for efficient memory management and accessing array elements. In this section, we will explore the relationship between pointers and multidimensional arrays.

6.4.1 Overview of Multidimensional Arrays

A multidimensional array is a collection of elements organized in multiple dimensions. The most common type is the two-dimensional array, which can be thought of as a table with rows and columns. In C, a two-dimensional array is declared as follows:

```
int matrix[3][4];
```

This declaration creates a 3x4 matrix of integers. The array elements can be accessed using indices, e.g., `matrix[1][2]` refers to the element in the second row and third column.

6.4.2 Memory Layout of Multidimensional Arrays

The memory of a multidimensional array is contiguous, and the elements are stored in row-major order. For a 3x4 matrix, the elements are stored in memory as if it were a one-dimensional array of size 12.

$$\begin{bmatrix} \text{matrix[0][0]} & \text{matrix[0][1]} & \text{matrix[0][2]} & \text{matrix[0][3]} \\ \text{matrix[1][0]} & \text{matrix[1][1]} & \text{matrix[1][2]} & \text{matrix[1][3]} \\ \text{matrix[2][0]} & \text{matrix[2][1]} & \text{matrix[2][2]} & \text{matrix[2][3]} \end{bmatrix}$$

6.4.3 Pointers to Multidimensional Arrays

A pointer to a multidimensional array in C is a complex concept. To declare a pointer to a two-dimensional array, we use the following syntax:

```
int (*ptr)[4];
```

Here, `ptr` is a pointer to an array of 4 integers. It can point to the entire array or to a specific row of the array.

```
#include <stdio.h>
```

```c
int main() {
    int matrix[3][4] = {
        {1, 2, 3, 4},
        {5, 6, 7, 8},
        {9, 10, 11, 12}
    };

    // Pointer to the entire array
    int (*ptrToMatrix)[4] = matrix;

    // Accessing elements using the pointer
    printf("Element at matrix[1][2]: %d\n", ptrToMatrix[1][2]);

    return 0;
}
```

In this example, `ptrToMatrix` is a pointer to the entire 3x4 array, and we use it to access a specific element.

6.4.4   Pointer Arithmetic with Multidimensional Arrays

Pointer arithmetic with multidimensional arrays involves understanding the size of each element and the number of elements in each dimension. When incrementing a pointer to a multidimensional array, it jumps to the next element based on the size of the array.

```c
#include <stdio.h>

int main() {
    int matrix[3][4] = {
        {1, 2, 3, 4},
        {5, 6, 7, 8},
```

```
        {9, 10, 11, 12}
    };

    // Pointer to the first row
    int *rowPtr = matrix[0];

    // Accessing elements using pointer arithmetic
    printf("Element at matrix[2][1]: %d\n", *(rowPtr + 2 * 4 + 1));

    return 0;
}
```

Here, `rowPtr` is a pointer to the first row, and we use pointer arithmetic to access the element at `matrix[2][1]`.

6.4.5 Dynamic Allocation of Multidimensional Arrays

Dynamic allocation of multidimensional arrays involves using pointers and `malloc()` or `calloc()` to allocate memory. The pointer manipulation is slightly more complex than with one-dimensional arrays.

```
#include <stdio.h>
#include <stdlib.h>

int main() {
    int **matrix;
    int rows = 3, cols = 4;

    // Allocate memory for rows
    matrix = (int **)malloc(rows * sizeof(int *));

    // Allocate memory for each row
```

```c
    for (int i = 0; i < rows; i++) {
        matrix[i] = (int *)malloc(cols * sizeof(int));
    }


    // Assign values to the elements
    for (int i = 0; i < rows; i++) {
        for (int j = 0; j < cols; j++) {
            matrix[i][j] = i * cols + j + 1;
        }
    }


    // Accessing elements
    printf("Element at matrix[2][1]: %d\n", matrix[2][1]);


    // Free allocated memory
    for (int i = 0; i < rows; i++) {
        free(matrix[i]);
    }
    free(matrix);


    return 0;
}
```

In this example, `matrix` is a pointer to a pointer, and dynamic allocation is done for both rows and columns.

6.4.6   Numerical Example: Matrix Multiplication

Matrix multiplication is a common application of multidimensional arrays. In this numerical example, we'll perform matrix multiplication using pointers.

```c
#include <stdio.h>
```

```
void multiplyMatrices(int firstMatrix[][3], int secondMatrix[][4], int result[][4]) {
    for (int i = 0; i < 3; ++i) {
        for (int j = 0; j < 4; ++j) {
            result[i][j] = 0;

            for (int k = 0; k < 3; ++k) {
                result[i][j] += firstMatrix[i][k] * secondMatrix[k][j];
            }
        }
    }
}


int main() {
    int firstMatrix[3][3] = {
        {1, 2, 3},
        {4, 5, 6},
        {7, 8, 9}
    };

    int secondMatrix[3][4] = {
        {1, 2, 3, 4},
        {5, 6, 7, 8},
        {9, 10, 11, 12}
    };

    int resultMatrix[3][4];

    multiplyMatrices(firstMatrix, secondMatrix, resultMatrix);

    // Displaying the multiplication result
```

```
    for (int i = 0; i < 3; ++i) {
        for (int j = 0; j < 4; ++j) {
            printf("%d\t", resultMatrix[i][j]);
            if (j == 3)
                printf("\n");
        }
    }


    return 0;
}
```

In this example, we define a function `multiplyMatrices` that performs matrix multiplication using pointers to two-dimensional arrays.

6.4.7   Best Practices and Considerations

When working with pointers and multidimensional arrays, consider the following:

1. **Pointer Initialization:** Ensure proper initialization of pointers to multidimensional arrays to avoid segmentation faults. 2. **Memory Management:** Be mindful of dynamic memory allocation and deallocation to prevent memory leaks. 3. **Pointer Arithmetic:** Use pointer arithmetic cautiously, keeping track of the size and dimensions of the array. 4. **Code Readability:** Provide comments and documentation, especially when dealing with complex pointer manipulations.

By mastering the interaction between pointers and multidimensional arrays, programmers can efficiently manipulate and manage data in a variety of applications.

Chapter 7

Pointers and File Handling

7.1 File Pointers

File pointers in C play a crucial role in handling files, reading data, and writing data. Understanding how file pointers work is essential for efficient file operations. In this section, we will explore the concept of file pointers and their application in C programming.

7.1.1 Overview of File Pointers

A file pointer is a pointer variable in C used to keep track of the current position within a file. It points to the next byte to be read or written in the file. File pointers are essential when performing various file operations such as reading, writing, and seeking within a file.

7.1.2 File Pointer Declaration

To declare a file pointer in C, we use the `FILE` data type provided by the standard input/output library (`stdio.h`). The general syntax is as follows:

```
FILE *filePointer;
```

127

Here, `filePointer` is a pointer to a `FILE` structure.

7.1.3 Opening and Closing Files

File pointers are commonly used to open and close files. The `fopen()` function is used to open a file, and the `fclose()` function is used to close it.

```
#include <stdio.h>

int main() {
    FILE *filePointer;

    // Opening a file in read mode
    filePointer = fopen("example.txt", "r");

    // Checking if file opened successfully
    if (filePointer == NULL) {
        printf("Unable to open file.\n");
        return 1; // Exit with an error code
    }

    // File operations go here

    // Closing the file
    fclose(filePointer);

    return 0;
}
```

In this example, the file "example.txt" is opened in read mode (`\r"`). It is important to check if the file opened successfully before performing any operations.

7.1.4 Reading from a File

File pointers are used to read data from a file. The `fscanf()` function is commonly used for reading formatted data from a file.

```c
#include <stdio.h>

int main() {
    FILE *filePointer;
    int data;

    filePointer = fopen("numbers.txt", "r");

    if (filePointer == NULL) {
        printf("Unable to open file.\n");
        return 1;
    }

    // Reading an integer from the file
    fscanf(filePointer, "%d", &data);

    // Displaying the read data
    printf("Read data: %d\n", data);

    fclose(filePointer);

    return 0;
}
```

In this example, an integer is read from the file "numbers.txt" using `fscanf()`.

7.1.5   Writing to a File

File pointers are also used to write data to a file. The `fprintf()` function is commonly used for writing formatted data to a file.

```c
#include <stdio.h>

int main() {
    FILE *filePointer;

    filePointer = fopen("output.txt", "w");

    if (filePointer == NULL) {
        printf("Unable to open file.\n");
        return 1;
    }

    // Writing data to the file
    fprintf(filePointer, "Hello, File!");

    fclose(filePointer);

    return 0;
}
```

In this example, the string "Hello, File!" is written to the file "output.txt" using `fprintf()`.

7.1.6   File Positioning with fseek()

The `fseek()` function is used to move the file pointer to a specific position within the file. This is useful for random access and updating specific parts of a file.

```c
#include <stdio.h>

int main() {
    FILE *filePointer;

    filePointer = fopen("data.bin", "rb");

    if (filePointer == NULL) {
        printf("Unable to open file.\n");
        return 1;
    }

    // Moving the file pointer to the 10th byte
    fseek(filePointer, 10, SEEK_SET);

    // File operations go here

    fclose(filePointer);

    return 0;
}
```

In this example, `fseek()` is used to move the file pointer to the 10th byte from the beginning of the file.

7.1.7 Numerical Example: Calculating File Size

A common application of file pointers is calculating the size of a file. This involves moving the file pointer to the end of the file using `fseek()` and then using `ftell()` to determine the file size.

```c
#include <stdio.h>
```

```
int main() {
    FILE *filePointer;
    long fileSize;

    filePointer = fopen("data.txt", "rb");

    if (filePointer == NULL) {
        printf("Unable to open file.\n");
        return 1;
    }

    // Move to the end of the file
    fseek(filePointer, 0, SEEK_END);

    // Get the current position (which is the file size)
    fileSize = ftell(filePointer);

    // Displaying the file size
    printf("File size: %ld bytes\n", fileSize);

    fclose(filePointer);

    return 0;
}
```

In this example, the file size of "data.txt" is calculated using file pointers.

7.1.8   Best Practices and Considerations

When working with file pointers in C, consider the following best practices:

    1. **Error Handling:** Always check if a file is opened successfully before

performing file operations. 2. **Closing Files:** Remember to close files after performing operations to free up system resources. 3. **File Positioning:** Use `fseek()` carefully to position the file pointer accurately. 4. **Efficient Reading and Writing:** Minimize the number of file read and write operations for efficiency.

By mastering file pointers, programmers can effectively manipulate files, read data, and perform various file operations in C.

7.2 Reading and Writing Files with Pointers

In C programming, reading and writing files using pointers provides a powerful mechanism for efficient and flexible file operations. Pointers allow direct access to memory, enabling optimized file handling. This section explores the techniques of reading and writing files using pointers and provides practical examples.

7.2.1 Reading Files with Pointers

To read a file using pointers, we leverage the `fread()` function. This function reads a specified number of elements from a file and stores them in memory. Pointers play a crucial role in efficiently managing the read data.

Consider the following example that reads integers from a binary file using pointers:

```
#include <stdio.h>

int main() {
    FILE *filePointer;
    int data[5]; // Assuming there are 5 integers in the file

    filePointer = fopen("numbers.bin", "rb");
```

```
if (filePointer == NULL) {

    printf("Unable to open file.\n");

    return 1;

}


// Reading integers from the file using fread()

fread(data, sizeof(int), 5, filePointer);


// Displaying the read data

for (int i = 0; i < 5; ++i) {

    printf("%d ", data[i]);

}


fclose(filePointer);


return 0;

}
```

In this example, an array of integers is used to store the data read from the binary file. The `fread()` function reads 5 integers from the file into the array.

7.2.2   Writing Files with Pointers

Similarly, writing files using pointers involves the `fwrite()` function. This function writes a specified number of elements from memory to a file. Pointers facilitate efficient management of the data to be written.

Consider the following example that writes integers to a binary file using pointers:

```
#include <stdio.h>


int main() {
```

```
    FILE *filePointer;
    int data[] = {1, 2, 3, 4, 5}; // Data to be written

    filePointer = fopen("output.bin", "wb");

    if (filePointer == NULL) {
        printf("Unable to open file.\n");
        return 1;
    }

    // Writing integers to the file using fwrite()
    fwrite(data, sizeof(int), 5, filePointer);

    fclose(filePointer);

    return 0;
}
```

In this example, the array `data` contains integers that will be written to the binary file using the `fwrite()` function.

7.2.3   Numerical Example: Efficient File Copy

An efficient file copy operation can be implemented using pointers. By dynamically allocating memory based on the file size and copying the entire file into memory, we can achieve faster file copying.

Consider the following example:

```
#include <stdio.h>
#include <stdlib.h>

int main() {
```

```
FILE *sourceFile, *destinationFile;
long fileSize;
char *buffer;


sourceFile = fopen("source.txt", "rb");


if (sourceFile == NULL) {
    printf("Unable to open source file.\n");
    return 1;
}


// Get the size of the source file
fseek(sourceFile, 0, SEEK_END);
fileSize = ftell(sourceFile);
fseek(sourceFile, 0, SEEK_SET);


// Allocate memory to store the entire file
buffer = (char *)malloc(fileSize);


// Read the entire file into the buffer
fread(buffer, 1, fileSize, sourceFile);


fclose(sourceFile);


destinationFile = fopen("copy.txt", "wb");


if (destinationFile == NULL) {
    printf("Unable to open destination file.\n");
    free(buffer);
    return 1;
}
```

```
// Write the buffer content to the destination file
fwrite(buffer, 1, fileSize, destinationFile);


fclose(destinationFile);
free(buffer);


printf("File copy successful.\n");


return 0;
}
```

In this example, the entire source file is read into a dynamically allocated buffer using pointers, and then the buffer is written to the destination file.

7.2.4 Best Practices and Considerations

When reading and writing files with pointers, consider the following best practices:

1. **Memory Management:** Dynamically allocate memory based on the file size for efficient operations. 2. **Error Handling:** Check for errors when opening, reading, and writing files to ensure robust file handling. 3. **File Copying:** For large file copying, use dynamic memory allocation to avoid memory limitations. 4. **Optimization:** Leverage pointers for direct access to memory, optimizing file operations.

By mastering the techniques of reading and writing files with pointers, programmers can enhance the performance and efficiency of file handling in C.

7.3 Error Handling in File Operations

Effective error handling is crucial when dealing with file operations in C. File operations can encounter various issues, such as file not found, permission errors, or unexpected file content. This section explores the importance of error handling and provides examples of how to handle errors in file operations using pointers.

7.3.1   Error Handling Basics

Error handling in file operations involves checking for potential issues and responding appropriately. Common file-related functions return NULL or specific error codes when errors occur. By checking these return values, a program can take corrective actions.

Consider the following example, where error handling is applied to file opening:

```
#include <stdio.h>

int main() {
    FILE *filePointer;

    // Attempting to open a file
    filePointer = fopen("nonexistent.txt", "r");

    // Checking if the file opened successfully
    if (filePointer == NULL) {
        printf("Error opening file. Check if the file exists.\n");
        return 1;
    }

    // File operations go here

    // Closing the file
    fclose(filePointer);
```

```
    return 0;
}
```

In this example, if the file "nonexistent.txt" does not exist, the `fopen()` function returns NULL, and an error message is displayed.

7.3.2 Handling File Read Errors

Reading data from a file can encounter errors, especially if the file content does not match the expected format. The `feof()` function is often used to check for the end of the file, and `ferror()` can be used to detect read errors.

Consider the following example:

```
#include <stdio.h>

int main() {
    FILE *filePointer;
    int data;

    filePointer = fopen("corrupted.txt", "r");

    if (filePointer == NULL) {
        printf("Error opening file.\n");
        return 1;
    }

    // Reading an integer from the file
    if (fscanf(filePointer, "%d", &data) == EOF) {
        if (feof(filePointer)) {
            printf("End of file reached.\n");
        } else if (ferror(filePointer)) {
            printf("Error reading from file.\n");
```

```
        }
    } else {
        // Successfully read data
        printf("Read data: %d\n", data);
    }


    fclose(filePointer);


    return 0;
}
```

In this example, if an error occurs during the read operation, `feof()` and `ferror()` are used to identify the cause.

7.3.3   Numerical Example: Safe File Copy with Error Handling

Building on the previous file copy example, let's enhance it with error handling to address potential issues during file operations.

```
#include <stdio.h>
#include <stdlib.h>


int main() {
    FILE *sourceFile, *destinationFile;
    long fileSize;
    char *buffer;


    sourceFile = fopen("source.txt", "rb");


    if (sourceFile == NULL) {
        perror("Error opening source file");
```

```
    return 1;
}

fseek(sourceFile, 0, SEEK_END);
fileSize = ftell(sourceFile);
fseek(sourceFile, 0, SEEK_SET);

buffer = (char *)malloc(fileSize);

if (buffer == NULL) {
    perror("Memory allocation error");
    fclose(sourceFile);
    return 2;
}

fread(buffer, 1, fileSize, sourceFile);

if (ferror(sourceFile)) {
    perror("Error reading from source file");
    fclose(sourceFile);
    free(buffer);
    return 3;
}

fclose(sourceFile);

destinationFile = fopen("copy.txt", "wb");

if (destinationFile == NULL) {
    perror("Error opening destination file");
    free(buffer);
```

```
        return 4;
    }


    fwrite(buffer, 1, fileSize, destinationFile);


    if (ferror(destinationFile)) {
        perror("Error writing to destination file");
        fclose(destinationFile);
        free(buffer);
        return 5;
    }


    fclose(destinationFile);
    free(buffer);


    printf("File copy successful.\n");


    return 0;
}
```

In this example, error handling is applied at various points during file operations, addressing potential issues during file opening, memory allocation, reading, and writing.

7.3.4   Best Practices for Error Handling

When handling errors in file operations, follow these best practices:

1. **Use `perror()`:** The `perror()` function prints a descriptive error message to the standard error stream, providing useful information about the last error that occurred.

2. **Check Return Values:** Always check the return values of file-related functions for `NULL` or error codes.

3. **Identify Error Types:** Use `feof()` and `ferror()` to differentiate between end-of-file and read/write errors.

4. **Clean Up Resources:** Properly close files and free allocated memory when errors occur to avoid resource leaks.

By implementing robust error handling, a C program can gracefully handle unexpected situations during file operations, ensuring more reliable and resilient file handling.

Chapter 8

Pointers and Data Structures

8.1 Linked Lists

Linked lists are fundamental data structures that leverage pointers to organize and manage data dynamically. Unlike arrays, linked lists provide flexibility in size, efficient insertions and deletions, and dynamic memory allocation. This section explores the concepts of linked lists, their implementation, and key operations.

8.1.1 Overview of Linked Lists

A linked list is a collection of nodes where each node contains data and a reference (pointer) to the next node in the sequence. The last node typically points to NULL, indicating the end of the list. The fundamental components of a linked list are:

- **Node:** Represents a single element in the list.

- **Data:** The information stored in each node.

• **Next Pointer:** A reference to the next node in the sequence.

The structure of a basic node in a singly linked list is represented as:

```
struct Node {    int data;    struct Node* next;};
```

8.1.2   Singly Linked List Implementation

Let's consider the implementation of a singly linked list in C. The following example demonstrates the creation of a linked list, insertion of nodes, and traversal:

```
#include <stdio.h>
#include <stdlib.h>

// Node structure
struct Node {
    int data;
    struct Node* next;
};


// Function to insert a new node at the beginning of the list
void insertAtBeginning(struct Node** head, int newData) {
    struct Node* newNode = (struct Node*)malloc(sizeof(struct Node));
    newNode->data = newData;
    newNode->next = *head;
    *head = newNode;
}


// Function to traverse and print the linked list
void printList(struct Node* head) {
    struct Node* current = head;
```

```
    while (current != NULL) {
        printf("%d -> ", current->data);
        current = current->next;
    }
    printf("NULL\n");
}


int main() {
    struct Node* head = NULL; // Initialize an empty list

    // Insert nodes at the beginning
    insertAtBeginning(&head, 3);
    insertAtBeginning(&head, 7);
    insertAtBeginning(&head, 9);

    // Print the linked list
    printf("Linked List: ");
    printList(head);

    return 0;
}
```

In this example, nodes are inserted at the beginning of the linked list, and the list is then printed.

8.1.3 Key Operations on Linked Lists

Linked lists support various operations, including insertion, deletion, and traversal. Some key operations include:

- **Insertion:** Nodes can be inserted at the beginning, end, or at a specific position in the list.

- **Deletion:** Nodes can be removed based on the value or position in the list.

- **Traversal:** Iterating through the list to access and manipulate nodes.

These operations are essential for building and maintaining linked lists in practical applications.

8.1.4   Numerical Example: Insertion in Sorted Order

Consider the scenario where nodes need to be inserted in sorted order. The following C code illustrates the insertion of nodes in a sorted singly linked list:

```c
#include <stdio.h>
#include <stdlib.h>

// Node structure
struct Node {
    int data;
    struct Node* next;
};

// Function to insert a new node in sorted order
void insertInSortedOrder(struct Node** head, int newData) {
    struct Node* newNode = (struct Node*)malloc(sizeof(struct Node));
    newNode->data = newData;
    newNode->next = NULL;

    // If the list is empty or the new node's data is less than the head
    if (*head == NULL || newData < (*head)->data) {
        newNode->next = *head;
        *head = newNode;
    } else {
```

```c
        struct Node* current = *head;

        // Traverse the list to find the correct position
        while (current->next != NULL && current->next->data < newData) {
            current = current->next;
        }

        // Insert the new node
        newNode->next = current->next;
        current->next = newNode;
    }
}


// Function to traverse and print the linked list
void printList(struct Node* head) {
    struct Node* current = head;
    while (current != NULL) {
        printf("%d -> ", current->data);
        current = current->next;
    }
    printf("NULL\n");
}


int main() {
    struct Node* head = NULL; // Initialize an empty list

    // Insert nodes in sorted order
    insertInSortedOrder(&head, 5);
    insertInSortedOrder(&head, 2);
    insertInSortedOrder(&head, 8);
```

```
// Print the linked list
printf("Sorted Linked List: ");
printList(head);

    return 0;
}
```

In this example, nodes are inserted in sorted order, ensuring that the linked list remains sorted after each insertion.

8.1.5   Best Practices and Considerations

When working with linked lists, consider the following best practices:

- **Memory Management:** Properly allocate and free memory for nodes to avoid memory leaks.

- **Traversal:** Use iterative or recursive methods for traversing linked lists based on the specific requirements.

- **Error Handling:** Check for memory allocation errors and handle them appropriately.

- **Encapsulation:** Encapsulate linked list operations in functions to enhance modularity and reusability.

By mastering linked list concepts and implementations, programmers can leverage this dynamic data structure to efficiently manage and manipulate data in various applications.

8.2   Trees

Trees are hierarchical data structures that use pointers to organize and represent data in a hierarchical manner. In the context of computer science, trees play a vital role in various applications, including databases, file systems, and artificial intelligence. This section delves into the fundamentals of trees, their types, and key operations.

8.2.1 Overview of Trees

A tree is a collection of nodes connected by edges, forming a hierarchical structure. The topmost node is called the root, and each node in the tree has a parent-child relationship with other nodes. The nodes in a tree can have zero or more children, but each node (except the root) has exactly one parent.

The fundamental components of a tree are:

- **Node:** Represents a single element in the tree.

- **Root:** The topmost node in the tree.

- **Parent:** A node that has one or more children.

- **Child:** A node that has a parent.

- **Leaf:** A node with no children.

The structure of a basic node in a binary tree is represented as:

```
struct TreeNode {
    int data;
    struct TreeNode* left;
    struct TreeNode* right;
};
```

8.2.2 Binary Trees

A binary tree is a type of tree in which each node has at most two children, referred to as the left child and the right child. Binary trees are commonly used in various algorithms and applications. Let's explore the implementation of a binary tree in C with an example:

```c
#include <stdio.h>
#include <stdlib.h>

// Node structure for a binary tree
struct TreeNode {
    int data;
    struct TreeNode* left;
    struct TreeNode* right;
};

// Function to create a new node
struct TreeNode* createNode(int newData) {
    struct TreeNode* newNode = (struct
    TreeNode*)malloc(sizeof(struct TreeNode));
    newNode->data = newData;
    newNode->left = NULL;
    newNode->right = NULL;
    return newNode;
}

int main() {
    // Creating a sample binary tree
    struct TreeNode* root = createNode(1);
    root->left = createNode(2);
    root->right = createNode(3);
    root->left->left = createNode(4);
    root->left->right = createNode(5);

    // Additional operations on the binary tree can
    be performed here
```

```
    return 0;
}
```

In this example, a binary tree is created with nodes containing integer data.

8.2.3 Tree Traversal

Tree traversal involves visiting each node in the tree exactly once to process or print its data. There are two primary methods for tree traversal:

- **Depth-First Traversal:** In-depth-first traversal, nodes are visited starting from the root, going as far as possible along each branch before backtracking. The three main types of depth-first traversal are in-order, pre-order, and post-order.

- **Breadth-First Traversal:** In breadth-first traversal, nodes are visited level by level, starting from the root and moving horizontally across each level before moving to the next level.

Let's consider an example of in-order traversal of a binary tree:

```c
#include <stdio.h>
#include <stdlib.h>

// Node structure for a binary tree
struct TreeNode {
    int data;
    struct TreeNode* left;
    struct TreeNode* right;
};

// Function for in-order traversal
void inOrderTraversal(struct TreeNode* root) {
    if (root != NULL) {
```

```c
        inOrderTraversal(root->left);

        printf("%d ", root->data);

        inOrderTraversal(root->right);

    }

}


int main() {

    // Creating a sample binary tree

    struct TreeNode* root = createNode(1);

    root->left = createNode(2);

    root->right = createNode(3);

    root->left->left = createNode(4);

    root->left->right = createNode(5);


    // In-order traversal

    printf("In-Order Traversal: ");

    inOrderTraversal(root);

    printf("\n");


    return 0;

}
```

In this example, the in-order traversal of the binary tree results in the sequence 4 2 5 1 3.

8.2.4   Numerical Example: Binary Search Tree (BST)

A binary search tree is a binary tree with the property that for each node, the values of all nodes in its left subtree are less than its value, and the values of all nodes in its right subtree are greater than its value. This property makes binary search trees efficient for searching, insertion, and deletion.

Consider the following C code for inserting nodes into a binary search tree:

```c
#include <stdio.h>
#include <stdlib.h>

// Node structure for a binary search tree
struct TreeNode {
    int data;
    struct TreeNode* left;
    struct TreeNode* right;
};


// Function to insert a new node into a binary search tree
struct TreeNode* insertNode(struct TreeNode* root, int newData) {
    if (root == NULL) {
        return createNode(newData);
    }


    // Recursively insert into the appropriate subtree
    if (newData < root->data) {
        root->left = insertNode(root->left, newData);
    } else if (newData > root->data) {
        root->right = insertNode(root->right, newData);
    }


    return root;
}


int main() {
    struct TreeNode* root = NULL; // Initialize an empty binary search tree

    // Insert nodes into the binary search tree
    root = insertNode(root, 50);
```

```
    root = insertNode(root, 30);
    root = insertNode(root, 20);
    root = insertNode(root, 40);
    root = insertNode(root, 70);
    root = insertNode(root, 60);
    root = insertNode(root, 80);


    // Additional operations on the binary search
    tree can be performed here


    return 0;
}
```

In this example, nodes are inserted into a binary search tree while maintaining the binary search tree property.

8.2.5   Best Practices and Considerations

When working with trees, consider the following best practices:

- **Memory Management:** Properly allocate and free memory for nodes to avoid memory leaks.

- **Traversal Techniques:** Choose the appropriate traversal technique (in-order, pre-order, post-order, or breadth-first) based on the requirements of the application.

- **Balanced Trees:** For efficiency, aim for balanced trees to ensure optimal performance in search, insertion, and deletion operations.

- **Binary Search Trees:** Utilize binary search trees for efficient searching in sorted data.

By understanding the principles of trees and their implementation, programmers can effectively model and manage hierarchical data structures in diverse applications.

8.3 Graphs

Graphs are versatile data structures that model relationships between entities. They consist of vertices (nodes) connected by edges. In computer science, graphs find applications in diverse areas such as social network analysis, network routing, and resource allocation. This section explores the basics of graphs, their types, and key operations.

8.3.1 Overview of Graphs

A graph G is defined as a pair (V, E), where V is the set of vertices and E is the set of edges. Each edge e in E connects two vertices in V, and it may have an associated weight or cost.

Types of Graphs

Graphs can be categorized into various types based on their properties:

- **Undirected Graph:** A graph in which edges have no direction. The edge (u, v) is identical to (v, u).

- **Directed Graph (Digraph):** A graph in which edges have a direction. The edge (u, v) is distinct from (v, u).

- **Weighted Graph:** A graph in which each edge has an associated weight or cost.

- **Cyclic Graph:** A graph that contains at least one cycle (a closed path).

- **Acyclic Graph:** A graph without any cycles.

8.3.2   Adjacency Matrix and Adjacency List

Two common representations of graphs are the adjacency matrix and the adjacency list.

Adjacency Matrix

An adjacency matrix M is a square matrix of size $|V| \times |V|$, where $|V|$ is the number of vertices. The entry $M[u][v]$ is 1 if there is an edge between vertices u and v, and 0 otherwise. For weighted graphs, $M[u][v]$ can represent the weight of the edge.

$$\begin{bmatrix} 0 & 1 & 0 & 1 \\ 1 & 0 & 1 & 1 \\ 0 & 1 & 0 & 0 \\ 1 & 1 & 0 & 0 \end{bmatrix}$$

Adjacency List

An adjacency list is a collection of lists or arrays, where each list represents the neighbors of a vertex. For example:

$$1 : \{2, 4\}$$
$$2 : \{1, 3, 4\}$$
$$3 : \{2\}$$
$$4 : \{1, 2\}$$

In the above representation, vertex 1 is connected to vertices 2 and 4.

8.3.3   Graph Traversal: Depth-First Search (DFS)

Depth-First Search (DFS) is a graph traversal algorithm that explores as far as possible along each branch before backtracking. It uses a stack or recursion to maintain the order of exploration.

Consider the following C code for DFS traversal of an undirected graph:

```c
#include <stdio.h>
#include <stdlib.h>

#define MAX_VERTICES 100

struct Graph {
    int vertices;
    int adjacencyMatrix[MAX_VERTICES][MAX_VERTICES];
};

void dfs(struct Graph* graph, int vertex, int visited[]) {
    printf("%d ", vertex);
    visited[vertex] = 1;

    for (int i = 0; i < graph->vertices; i++) {
        if (graph->adjacencyMatrix[vertex][i] && !visited[i]) {
            dfs(graph, i, visited);
        }
    }
}

int main() {
    struct Graph sampleGraph = {4, {{0, 1, 0, 1},
                                    {1, 0, 1, 1},
                                    {0, 1, 0, 0},
                                    {1, 1, 0, 0}}};

    int visited[MAX_VERTICES] = {0};
```

```
    printf("DFS Traversal: ");
    dfs(&sampleGraph, 0, visited);

    return 0;
}
```

In this example, DFS traversal starts from vertex 0, visiting connected vertices in depth-first order.

8.3.4   Numerical Example: Dijkstra's Algorithm

Dijkstra's Algorithm is a widely used algorithm for finding the shortest paths between nodes in a weighted graph. The algorithm maintains a set of vertices whose shortest distance from the source is known.

Consider the following C code for Dijkstra's Algorithm:

```
#include <stdio.h>
#include <limits.h>

#define MAX_VERTICES 100

struct Graph {
    int vertices;
    int adjacencyMatrix[MAX_VERTICES][MAX_VERTICES];
};

int minDistance(int distance[], int shortestPathSet[], int vertices) {
    int min = INT_MAX, minIndex;

    for (int v = 0; v < vertices; v++) {
        if (!shortestPathSet[v] && distance[v] <= min) {
```

```
            min = distance[v];
            minIndex = v;
        }
    }


    return minIndex;
}


void dijkstra(struct Graph* graph, int source) {
    int distance[MAX_VERTICES];
    int shortestPathSet[MAX_VERTICES];

    for (int i = 0; i < graph->vertices; i++) {
        distance[i] = INT_MAX;
        shortestPathSet[i] = 0;
    }


    distance[source] = 0;


    for (int count = 0; count < graph->vertices - 1; count++) {
        int u = minDistance(distance, shortestPathSet, graph->vertices);
        shortestPathSet[u] = 1;

        for (int v = 0; v < graph->vertices; v++) {
            if (!shortestPathSet[v] && graph->adjacencyMatrix[u][v] &&
                distance[u] != INT_MAX && distance[u]
                + graph->adjacencyMatrix[u][v] < distance[v]) {
                distance[v] = distance[u] + graph->adjacencyMatrix[u][v];
            }
        }
    }
```

```
    printf("Shortest Distances from Source %d:\n", source);
    for (int i = 0; i < graph->vertices; i++) {
        printf("Vertex %d: %d\n", i, distance[i]);
    }
}


int main() {
    struct Graph weightedGraph = {5, {{0, 2, 0, 6, 0},
                                      {2, 0, 3, 8, 5},
                                      {0, 3, 0, 0, 7},
                                      {6, 8, 0, 0, 9},
                                      {0, 5, 7, 9, 0}}};

    int sourceVertex = 0;
    dijkstra(&weightedGraph, sourceVertex);

    return 0;
}
```

In this example, Dijkstra's Algorithm finds the shortest distances from a source vertex to all other vertices in a weighted graph.

8.4   Pointers in Hash Tables

Hash tables are fundamental data structures that provide efficient data retrieval based on key-value pairs. They utilize a hash function to map keys to indices in an array, allowing for constant-time average case complexity for operations like insertion, deletion, and retrieval. Pointers play a crucial role in managing hash tables effectively.

8.4.1 Overview of Hash Tables

A hash table is an array that uses a hash function to map keys to indices. Each index in the array, often called a bucket, may store multiple key-value pairs. The goal is to distribute the keys uniformly across the array, minimizing collisions.

Hash Function

The hash function is a crucial component of a hash table. It takes a key as input and produces an index in the array where the corresponding value can be stored. A good hash function aims to distribute keys evenly to avoid collisions.

$$\text{index} = \text{hash\_function}(\text{key})$$

Collision Resolution

Collisions occur when two keys hash to the same index. There are various collision resolution techniques, including chaining (using linked lists in each bucket) and open addressing (finding the next available slot).

8.4.2 Pointers in Hash Table Implementation

Pointers are extensively used in the implementation of hash tables, especially when dealing with dynamic data structures like linked lists for collision resolution.

Structures in Hash Tables

In C, a typical structure for a hash table node might look like this:

```
struct Node {
    int key;
    int value;
    struct Node* next;
};
```

Here, **next** is a pointer to the next node in the linked list, which is used for chaining.

Hash Table Operations

Let's consider a basic example of inserting a key-value pair into a hash table using chaining for collision resolution:

```
#include <stdio.h>
#include <stdlib.h>

#define TABLE_SIZE 10

struct Node {
    int key;
    int value;
    struct Node* next;
};

struct Node* createNode(int key, int value) {
    struct Node* newNode = (struct Node*)malloc(sizeof(struct Node));
    newNode->key = key;
    newNode->value = value;
    newNode->next = NULL;
    return newNode;
}

void insert(struct Node* hashTable[], int key, int value) {
    int index = key % TABLE_SIZE;
    struct Node* newNode = createNode(key, value);

    if (hashTable[index] == NULL) {
```

```
        hashTable[index] = newNode;
    } else {
        // Chaining: add the new node to the beginning of the linked list
        newNode->next = hashTable[index];
        hashTable[index] = newNode;
    }
}


int main() {
    struct Node* hashTable[TABLE_SIZE] = {NULL};

    // Inserting key-value pairs
    insert(hashTable, 42, 100);
    insert(hashTable, 7, 200);
    insert(hashTable, 15, 300);

    // Additional operations on the hash table can be performed here

    return 0;
}
```

In this example, the `insert` function calculates the hash index, creates a new node, and inserts it into the hash table using chaining.

8.4.3 Numerical Example: Hashing Integers

Consider a simple example of a hash function for hashing integers:

$$hash\_function(key) = key \ \% \ TABLE\_SIZE$$

This hash function takes an integer key and returns the remainder when divided by the table size.

Chapter 9

Pointers and Performance Optimization

9.1 Pointer Efficiency

Efficient use of pointers is crucial for optimizing the performance of C programs. This section explores various strategies and techniques for leveraging pointers to enhance program efficiency.

9.1.1 Reducing Memory Footprint

One of the primary benefits of using pointers is the ability to reduce memory consumption. Consider a scenario where multiple variables of the same type are needed. Instead of declaring individual variables, pointers can be used to dynamically allocate memory, reducing the overall memory footprint.

$$\text{int *arr = (int *)malloc(sizeof(int) * size);}$$

Here, `arr` is a pointer to an integer array dynamically allocated based on the required size.

9.1.2   Pointer Arithmetic for Efficiency

Pointer arithmetic allows for efficient traversal of data structures like arrays. For instance, when iterating through an array, using pointer arithmetic is often faster than using array indices.

```
int *ptr = arr;
for (int i = 0; i < size; ++i) {
    printf("%d ", *ptr);
    ptr++;
}
```

In this example, `ptr` is initially set to the beginning of the array, and then it is incremented to move through the elements.

9.1.3   Function Pointers for Dynamic Behavior

Function pointers provide a mechanism for dynamic function calls, allowing the selection of functions at runtime. This can lead to more flexible and optimized code, especially in scenarios where different functions need to be called based on specific conditions.

```
int add(int a, int b) { return a + b; }
int subtract(int a, int b) { return a - b; }
int (*operation)(int, int);
operation = add;
printf("%d", operation(5, 3));
operation = subtract;
printf("%d", operation(5, 3));
```

In this example, the function pointer `operation` is dynamically assigned to either the `add` or `subtract` function based on program requirements.

9.1.4   Numerical Example: Optimizing Array Traversal

Consider a scenario where a large array needs to be traversed, and the goal is to optimize the traversal using pointer arithmetic:

```
int arr[1000000];
int *ptr = arr;
for (int i = 0; i < 1000000; ++i) {
    // Perform operations on *ptr
    ptr++;
}
```

By using pointer arithmetic, the loop can iterate through the array more efficiently than using array indices.

9.2   Tips for Optimizing Code with Pointers

Optimizing code with pointers is a critical aspect of C programming. This section provides practical tips and techniques for enhancing the performance of code through efficient use of pointers.

9.2.1   Minimize Dereferencing

Excessive dereferencing of pointers can introduce overhead. It's important to minimize unnecessary dereferencing, especially within loops or critical sections of code. Consider the following example:

$$\text{int value} = \text{*ptr;}$$

In this case, if the value pointed to by `ptr` is only used once, it might be more efficient to directly use `ptr` in subsequent operations.

9.2.2   Use const Correctly

The const qualifier can be used to indicate that a pointer or the data it points to should not be modified. Correctly applying const can enable the compiler to make optimizations and also make the code more readable and maintainable.

```
const int *readOnlyPtr;
int *const constantPtr;
const int *const readOnlyConstantPtr;
```

In these examples, readOnlyPtr indicates that the data it points to should not be modified, constantPtr indicates that the pointer itself is constant, and readOnlyConstantPtr combines both.

9.2.3   Avoid Unnecessary Memory Allocations

Dynamic memory allocation and deallocation can introduce overhead. Minimize unnecessary memory allocations, especially in performance-critical sections. Consider reusing memory where possible or using stack memory.

```
int array[100];
int *dynamicArray = (int *)malloc(sizeof(int) * 100);
```

In this example, if the array size is fixed, using a statically allocated array (int array[100];) may be more efficient.

9.2.4   Optimize Loop Iterations

When working with arrays or data structures, optimizing loop iterations can significantly impact performance. Consider using pointer arithmetic for array traversal and ensuring that loop conditions are efficiently structured.

```
int *ptr = array;
for (int i = 0; i < size; ++i) {
    // Operations using *ptr
```

```
    ptr++;
}
```

In this example, using pointer arithmetic for array traversal can be more efficient than using array indices.

9.2.5 Numerical Example: Minimizing Dereferencing Overhead

Consider the following code snippet where minimizing dereferencing overhead is applied:

```
int sum = 0;
for (int i = 0; i < size; ++i) {
    sum += *ptr;
    // Additional operations without dereferencing
    ptr++;
}
```

By using `sum += *ptr;` only once within the loop, unnecessary dereferencing overhead is minimized.

9.3 Common Pitfalls and How to Avoid Them

While pointers in C provide powerful capabilities, they also come with certain pitfalls that, if not handled correctly, can lead to bugs, memory leaks, and performance issues. This section highlights common pitfalls and provides guidance on how to avoid them.

9.3.1 Dangling Pointers

Dangling pointers occur when a pointer points to a memory location that has been deallocated or is no longer valid. Accessing or modifying data through a dangling pointer can result in undefined behavior. To avoid this, it's crucial to set pointers to NULL after freeing the memory they point to.

```
int *ptr = (int *)malloc(sizeof(int));
// Use ptr
free(ptr);
ptr = NULL;
```

In this example, setting `ptr` to NULL after `free` prevents it from becoming a dangling pointer.

9.3.2   Memory Leaks

Forgetting to free dynamically allocated memory leads to memory leaks. Always free memory using `free` when it is no longer needed.

```
int *ptr = (int *)malloc(sizeof(int));
// Use ptr
free(ptr); // Don't forget to free
```

In this example, failing to call `free` would result in a memory leak.

9.3.3   Uninitialized Pointers

Using uninitialized pointers can lead to undefined behavior. Always initialize pointers before use, either by assigning them a valid memory address or by setting them to NULL.

```
int *ptr = NULL;
// Use ptr safely
```

Here, `ptr` is initialized to NULL to avoid using it before assigning a valid address.

9.3.4 Incorrect Pointer Arithmetic

Incorrect use of pointer arithmetic, such as going beyond the bounds of an array, can result in undefined behavior and memory corruption. Always ensure that pointer arithmetic stays within the bounds of the allocated memory.

```
int arr[5];
int *ptr = arr;
// Ensure ptr stays within bounds
*(ptr + 5) = 10; // Incorrect
```

In this example, attempting to access `*(ptr + 5)` goes beyond the bounds of the array.

9.3.5 Numerical Example: Avoiding Dangling Pointers

Consider the following code snippet where dangling pointers are avoided:

```
int *ptr = (int *)malloc(sizeof(int));
// Use ptr
free(ptr);
ptr = NULL; // Avoids dangling pointer
```

By setting `ptr` to `NULL` after freeing the memory, the risk of it becoming a dangling pointer is mitigated.

Chapter 10

Pointers and Advanced C Programming Techniques

10.1 Pointers and Bit Manipulation

Bit manipulation is a powerful technique in C programming, and pointers can be utilized to perform efficient bit-level operations. This section explores how pointers can be used in conjunction with bit manipulation to achieve various tasks.

10.1.1 Bitwise Operators

C provides bitwise operators that operate on individual bits of integers. Pointers can be employed to manipulate specific bits within variables. The bitwise AND (&), OR (|), XOR (^), left shift (¡¡), and right shift (¿¿) operators are commonly used for this purpose.

```
int num = 5;
int *ptr = &num;
*ptr = *ptr & 3; // Clearing all bits except the two least significant bits
```

In this example, the two least significant bits of `num` are preserved, and the rest are cleared using the bitwise AND operator.

10.1.2 Bitwise Manipulation for Flags

Pointers can be employed to set, clear, toggle, or check individual bits that act as flags. This is often used in embedded systems programming and other scenarios where memory efficiency is crucial.

```
unsigned char flags = 0;
unsigned char *flagsPtr = &flags;
*flagsPtr = *flagsPtr | (1 << 2); // Set the third flag
```

Here, the third flag is set by performing a bitwise OR operation with a value that has the third bit set.

10.1.3 Bitwise Shifts and Pointers

Pointers can be used to shift bits efficiently, especially when dealing with large data structures or arrays of bits.

```
unsigned int bits = 0xFF;
unsigned int *bitsPtr = &bits;
*bitsPtr = *bitsPtr << 3; // Left shift by 3 bits
```

This example demonstrates left-shifting the bits in `bits` by 3 positions.

10.1.4 Manipulating Individual Bits

Pointers allow for the manipulation of individual bits within variables without affecting the other bits. This is particularly useful in scenarios where fine-grained control is required.

```
unsigned char data = 0x0A;
unsigned char *dataPtr = &data;
*dataPtr = *dataPtr ^ (1 << 1); // Toggle the second bit
```

Here, the second bit of `data` is toggled using the bitwise XOR operation.

10.1.5 Numerical Example: Bitwise Manipulation for Flags

Consider the following example where bitwise manipulation is used for flags:

```
unsigned char flags = 0;
unsigned char *flagsPtr = &flags;
*flagsPtr = *flagsPtr | (1 << 4); // Set the fifth flag
if (*flagsPtr & (1 << 4)) {
    // Fifth flag is set
}
```

In this example, the fifth flag is set, and later, it is checked using bitwise AND.

10.2 Pointers and Embedded Systems

Embedded systems often have stringent resource constraints, and understanding how to use pointers efficiently is crucial for programming these systems. This section delves into the role of pointers in embedded systems and provides practical examples.

10.2.1 Memory Constraints in Embedded Systems

Embedded systems typically operate with limited memory resources. Pointers become essential in managing memory efficiently, enabling precise control over data storage and retrieval.

10.2.2 Pointer-Based Data Structures

In embedded systems, memory efficiency is paramount. Pointers facilitate the implementation of data structures such as linked lists, trees, and queues, optimizing memory usage and ensuring quick access to data.

```
struct Node {
    int data;
    struct Node *next;
};
```

Here, a simple linked list node structure is defined. Such structures are commonly used in embedded systems for dynamic data management.

10.2.3 Accessing Hardware Registers

Embedded systems often involve interfacing with hardware through memory-mapped registers. Pointers can be used to directly access and modify these registers, providing a low-level interface.

```
volatile uint32_t *timerCtrl = (volatile uint32_t *)0x40000000;
*timerCtrl = 0x02; // Set control register to 0x02
```

In this example, a pointer is used to access and configure a timer control register at memory address 0x40000000.

10.2.4 Efficient Array Manipulation

Arrays are frequently used in embedded systems for storing sensor data, configuration parameters, etc. Pointers enable efficient array manipulation and traversal.

```
int sensorData[10];
int *sensorPtr = sensorData;
for (int i = 0; i < 10; i++) {
    sensorPtr[i] = i * 2; // Populate array with values
}
```

Here, a pointer is used to populate an array with values, showcasing a simple and memory-efficient approach.

10.2.5 Pointer Arithmetic in Embedded Systems

Pointer arithmetic is beneficial in embedded systems for navigating through memory efficiently. It allows precise control over memory addresses and facilitates optimizations.

```
int dataArray[5] = {10, 20, 30, 40, 50};
int *ptr = dataArray;
int sum = 0;
for (int i = 0; i < 5; i++) {
    sum += *(ptr + i); // Access array elements using pointer arithmetic
}
```

In this example, pointer arithmetic is used to calculate the sum of elements in an array.

10.2.6 Numerical Example: Controlling GPIO Pins

Consider a scenario where an embedded system needs to control GPIO pins. Pointers can be utilized to set, clear, or toggle individual bits corresponding to these pins.

```
volatile uint32_t *gpioPort = (volatile uint32_t *)0x40004000;
*gpioPort |= (1 << 5); // Set GPIO pin 5
```

Here, a pointer is used to access and set the state of GPIO pin 5 in a memory-mapped register.

10.3 Pointers and Low-Level Programming

Low-level programming involves interacting directly with the hardware and memory, and pointers are indispensable in this domain. This section explores the role of pointers in low-level programming, providing practical examples and insights.

10.3.1 Memory Management and Pointers

Low-level programming often requires precise control over memory. Pointers facilitate dynamic memory allocation and deallocation, enabling efficient use of resources.

$$\text{int *dynamicArray} = (\text{int *})\text{malloc}(5 * \text{sizeof(int)});$$

Here, dynamic memory allocation is performed using `malloc()`, and the resulting pointer, `dynamicArray`, can be used to access the allocated memory.

10.3.2 Manipulating Binary Data

Low-level programming frequently involves dealing with binary data. Pointers enable efficient manipulation of binary information by providing direct access to memory.

```
uint8_t binaryData[4] = {0xAB, 0xCD, 0x12, 0x34};
uint16_t *shortPtr = (uint16_t *)binaryData;
```

In this example, a pointer is used to interpret the binary data as a sequence of 16-bit values.

10.3.3 Direct Memory Access (DMA)

Pointers play a crucial role in DMA, allowing data to be transferred directly between peripherals and memory without CPU intervention.

```
volatile uint32_t *source = (volatile uint32_t *)0x40004000;
volatile uint32_t *destination = (volatile uint32_t *)0x20000000;
int size = 1024;
while (size--) {
    *destination++ = *source++;
}
```

This example demonstrates a simple DMA transfer where data is moved from a source memory location to a destination location using pointers.

10.3.4 Pointer to Function

In low-level programming, function pointers are powerful constructs. They allow dynamic selection and invocation of functions, providing flexibility in program execution.

```
int add(int a, int b) { return a + b; }
int (*functionPtr)(int, int) = add;
int result = (*functionPtr)(3, 5); // result will be 8
```

Here, a function pointer is declared and assigned the address of the add function, enabling dynamic function invocation.

10.3.5 Bit-Level Manipulation

Low-level programming often requires manipulation of individual bits in registers. Pointers can be used to directly access and modify bits.

```
volatile uint32_t *registerPtr = (volatile uint32_t *)0x40001000;
*registerPtr |= (1 << 3); // Set the 4th bit
```

In this example, a pointer is used to set the 4th bit of a memory-mapped register.

10.3.6 Numerical Example: Implementing a Memory Copy Function

Consider the implementation of a simple memory copy function using pointers. This low-level operation is foundational in systems programming.

```
void memoryCopy(void *dest, const void *src, size_t size) {
    char *destPtr = (char *)dest;
```

```
    const char *srcPtr = (const char *)src;
    while (size--) {
        *destPtr++ = *srcPtr++;
    }
}
```

This function takes pointers to source and destination memory locations and copies a specified number of bytes.

Chapter 11

Pointers in Real-world Applications

11.1 Case Studies

This section presents real-world case studies where pointers play a pivotal role in solving practical problems. Each case study is accompanied by working examples, numerical illustrations, and detailed explanations.

11.1.1 Case Study 1: Memory-efficient String Manipulation

In applications where memory efficiency is critical, optimizing string manipulation can be a key concern. Pointers offer a solution by enabling efficient string operations without unnecessary memory overhead.

Listing 11.1: Concatenate Strings

```
char *concatenateStrings(const char *str1, const char *str2) {
    size_t len1 = strlen(str1);
    size_t len2 = strlen(str2);
```

```c
char *result = (char *)malloc(len1 + len2 + 1);
if (result == NULL) {
    // Handle memory allocation failure
    return NULL;
}

strcpy(result, str1);
strcat(result, str2);

return result;
}
```

11.1.2   Case Study 2: Efficient Data Structures

Pointers are instrumental in implementing efficient data structures. Consider the case of a linked list:

Listing 11.2: Linked List Node

```c
struct Node {
    int data;
    struct Node *next;
};

struct Node *createNode(int data) {
    struct Node *newNode = (struct Node *)malloc(sizeof(struct Node));
    if (newNode == NULL) {
        // Handle memory allocation failure
        return NULL;
    }
```

```
newNode->data = data;
newNode->next = NULL;


return newNode;
}
```

11.1.3   Case Study 3: File Handling and Pointers

When dealing with large files, efficient file handling is crucial. Pointers can be
employed to optimize file operations.

Listing 11.3: Copy File

```
#include <stdio.h>


void copyFile(FILE *source, FILE *destination) {
    fseek(source, 0, SEEK_END);
    long fileSize = ftell(source);
    rewind(source);

    char *buffer = (char *)malloc(fileSize);
    if (buffer == NULL) {
        // Handle memory allocation failure
        return;
    }

    fread(buffer, 1, fileSize, source);
    fwrite(buffer, 1, fileSize, destination);

    free(buffer);
}
```

11.1.4   Case Study 4: Embedded Systems

In embedded systems, where resources are constrained, pointers are invaluable for optimizing code and managing hardware interfaces. For instance, consider a simple GPIO control:

Listing 11.4: GPIO Control in Embedded Systems

```
volatile uint32_t *gpioRegister = (volatile uint32_t *)0x40001000;
*gpioRegister |= (1 << 5); // Set the 6th bit for GPIO control
```

Here, a pointer facilitates direct access to a memory-mapped register, allowing efficient control over a GPIO pin.

11.2   Best Practices in Industrial Codebases

This section explores the best practices for using pointers in large-scale industrial codebases. Industrial applications demand robust, efficient, and maintainable code, and pointers play a crucial role in achieving these goals.

11.2.1   Pointer Usage Guidelines

In industrial settings, following certain guidelines for pointer usage is essential to ensure code reliability and readability. Here are some key practices:

1. **Document Pointer Semantics:** Clearly document the semantics and ownership rules of pointers. This includes specifying whether a function assumes ownership of a pointer or if it is merely borrowing it.

2. **Avoid Raw Pointers:** Minimize the use of raw pointers and prefer smart pointers or safer alternatives. Smart pointers in C++ (e.g., `std::shared_ptr`) help manage memory automatically and reduce the risk of memory leaks.

3. **Const-Correctness:** Enforce const-correctness to prevent unintended modifications through pointers. Use `const` qualifiers appropriately to indicate whether a pointer can modify the pointed-to data.

4. **Memory Safety:** Emphasize memory safety by validating pointers before dereferencing them. Perform thorough boundary checks and ensure that pointers are not used after the memory they point to has been deallocated.

11.2.2 Real-world Example: Memory Management in an Industrial Control System

Consider an industrial control system where memory management is critical for stability and performance. The following code snippet demonstrates a best practice for memory allocation in such systems:

Listing 11.5: Memory Allocation in Industrial Control System

```c
#include <stdlib.h>

// Function to allocate memory for sensor data
float *allocateSensorData(int numSensors) {
    // Allocate memory for sensor readings
    float *sensorData = (float *)malloc(numSensors * sizeof(float));

    if (sensorData == NULL) {
        // Handle memory allocation failure
        // Log an error or take appropriate action
    }

    return sensorData;
}
```

In this example, dynamic memory is allocated for sensor readings, and proper error handling is included to manage potential allocation failures.

11.2.3   Performance Optimization

In industrial codebases, performance is often a critical factor. Pointers can be leveraged for performance optimization through techniques such as caching and efficient data access.

11.3   Pointers and System-Level Programming

This section delves into the use of pointers in system-level programming, where direct memory manipulation and control are crucial. System-level programming often involves interfacing with hardware and managing low-level system resources.

11.3.1   Memory-Mapped I/O

One common scenario in system-level programming is the use of memory-mapped I/O to communicate with hardware peripherals. Pointers provide a direct and efficient way to access memory-mapped registers. Consider the following example:

Listing 11.6: Memory-Mapped I/O Using Pointers

```
#include <stdint.h>

// Define a structure representing a hardware register
typedef struct {
    volatile uint32_t control;
    volatile uint32_t data;
} HardwareDevice;

// Pointer to the base address of the hardware device
HardwareDevice *device = (HardwareDevice *)0x40000000;
```

```
int main() {
    // Access control register
    device->control = 0x1;

    // Write data to the device
    device->data = 0x12345678;

    // Perform other operations...

    return 0;
}
```

In this example, the `device` pointer is used to access the control and data registers of a hardware device.

11.3.2 Direct Memory Manipulation

System-level programming often requires direct manipulation of memory for tasks like memory copying, initialization, or low-level data processing. Pointers enable efficient memory operations, as shown in the following example:

Listing 11.7: Direct Memory Manipulation

```
#include <string.h>

int main() {
    // Source and destination buffers
    char source[] = "Hello, System!";
    char destination[20];

    // Pointer to the source and destination
    char *sourcePtr = source;
    char *destPtr = destination;
```

```
// Copy data from source to destination
while (*sourcePtr != '\0') {
    *destPtr = *sourcePtr;
    sourcePtr++;
    destPtr++;
}

// Null-terminate the destination string
*destPtr = '\0';

// Perform other operations...

    return 0;
}
```

In this example, pointers are used for efficient string copying without relying on standard library functions.

11.3.3 Numerical Examples

Consider the scenario of implementing a memory allocator for a system with constrained resources. Pointers play a key role in managing memory blocks and ensuring efficient allocation and deallocation.

Appendix A

Glossary of Terms

A.1 Definitions and Explanations of Key Terms Used in the Book

This section provides comprehensive definitions and explanations of key terms used throughout the book. Understanding these terms is crucial for grasping the concepts discussed in various chapters.

A.1.1 Pointer

A pointer is a variable that stores the memory address of another variable. It allows direct manipulation of memory and is a fundamental concept in C programming.

A.1.2 Dereferencing

Dereferencing a pointer means accessing the value stored at the memory address it points to. It is done using the '*' operator.

A.1.3   Memory-Mapped I/O

Memory-mapped I/O is a technique where hardware registers are treated as if they were memory locations. This allows direct interaction with hardware using pointers.

A.1.4   Dynamic Memory Allocation

Dynamic memory allocation involves allocating memory during program execution. Functions like `malloc()` and `free()` are used for this purpose.

A.1.5   Null Pointer

A null pointer is a pointer that does not point to any memory location. It is often used to signify the absence of a valid memory address.

A.1.6   Pointer Arithmetic

Pointer arithmetic involves performing arithmetic operations on pointers. It is commonly used for traversing arrays and manipulating memory.

A.1.7   Void Pointer

A void pointer is a pointer that has no associated data type. It can be used to point to objects of any type.

A.1.8   Function Pointer

A function pointer points to a function instead of a variable. It allows functions to be passed as arguments or returned from other functions.

A.1.9   File Pointer

In file handling, a file pointer is a pointer used to navigate and manipulate data in files. Functions like `fopen()` and `fclose()` are used with file pointers.

A.1.10 Linked List

A linked list is a data structure where elements are connected using pointers. It allows dynamic memory allocation and efficient insertion/deletion operations.

A.1.11 Binary Tree

A binary tree is a hierarchical data structure composed of nodes, each having at most two children. Pointers are used to establish connections between nodes.

A.1.12 Graph

In graph theory, a graph consists of nodes and edges. Pointers are used to represent connections between nodes in various graph algorithms.

A.1.13 Hash Table

A hash table is a data structure that uses a hash function to map keys to array indices. Pointers are used to manage collisions and navigate the table.

A.1.14 Pointer Efficiency

Pointer efficiency refers to writing code that maximizes the performance benefits of using pointers. It involves minimizing unnecessary operations and memory accesses.

A.1.15 Pointer Safety

Pointer safety ensures that pointers are used in a way that avoids memory-related errors such as segmentation faults and memory leaks.

A.1.16 Embedded Systems

Embedded systems are specialized computing systems designed for specific tasks. Pointers are extensively used in embedded programming for resource management.

A.1.17   Low-Level Programming

Low-level programming involves direct manipulation of hardware and memory. Pointers are essential for tasks like device driver development and system-level programming.

A.1.18   Bit Manipulation

Bit manipulation involves performing operations at the bit level. Pointers can be used for efficient bit-level operations in various applications.

A.1.19   System-Level Programming

System-level programming deals with tasks related to the operating system and hardware. Pointers are crucial for tasks like memory management and interfacing with hardware.

A.1.20   Performance Optimization

Performance optimization involves enhancing code efficiency. Pointers play a significant role in optimizing memory usage and execution speed.

A.1.21   Error Handling

Error handling in C involves using pointers to manage errors effectively. Proper use of pointers can prevent memory-related errors and improve program reliability.

A.1.22   Data Structures

Data structures like arrays, linked lists, and trees heavily rely on pointers for efficient storage and retrieval of data.

A.1.23 Real-world Applications

Pointers find applications in real-world scenarios such as networking, embedded systems, and performance-critical applications. Understanding pointers is crucial for writing robust and efficient code.

Appendix B

Quick Reference

B.1 Summary of Pointer Syntax and Operations

This section provides a concise summary of pointer syntax and operations in C. Understanding these fundamentals is essential for efficient use of pointers in your programs.

Pointer Declaration

A pointer is declared using the syntax:

```
type *pointer_name;
```

where **type** is the base data type and **pointer_name** is the name of the pointer.

Pointer Initialization

A pointer can be initialized using the address-of operator (&) with a variable:

```
int x = 10;  int *ptr = &x;
```

Dereferencing

Dereferencing a pointer means accessing the value it points to. Use the dereference operator (*):

$$\text{int value = *ptr;}$$

Pointer Arithmetic

Pointer arithmetic allows moving through memory. If `ptr` is a pointer, `ptr++` moves to the next memory location of its type.

Arrays and Pointers

Arrays and pointers are closely related. The name of an array is a pointer to its first element:

```
int arr[5] = {1, 2, 3, 4, 5};
int *ptr = arr;
```

Pointer to Functions

A pointer to a function allows calling a function indirectly. Syntax:

$$\text{int (*funcPtr)(int, int) = \&add;}$$

Void Pointer

A void pointer (`void *`) is a generic pointer that can point to any data type.

Dynamic Memory Allocation

Use `malloc()` for dynamic memory allocation:

$$\text{int *dynamicArray = (int *)malloc(5 * sizeof(int));}$$

Freeing Allocated Memory

Use `free()` to deallocate memory:

```
free(dynamicArray);
```

Pointers and Structures

Structures can be accessed through pointers:

```
struct Point { int x, y; };  struct Point p; struct Point *ptr = &p;
```

Pointer to Pointer

A pointer to a pointer (`int **`) holds the address of another pointer.

Function Pointers

A pointer to a function can be used to call different functions dynamically.

File Pointers

File pointers (`FILE *`) are used for file handling operations:

```
FILE *filePtr = fopen(\example.txt", \r");
```

Error Handling

Check for null pointers to handle errors effectively.

Linked List and Pointers

Linked lists are implemented using pointers to connect nodes.

Bit Manipulation

Pointers can be used for efficient bit-level operations.

Performance Optimization

Optimize code by minimizing unnecessary pointer operations.

System-Level Programming

Pointers are crucial for system-level programming tasks.

Best Practices

Follow best practices to ensure safe and efficient use of pointers in your programs.

Index

This chapter serves as an index, providing a quick reference to key terms and concepts covered throughout the book.

Index of Key Terms

- **Pointer Declaration:** The syntax for declaring a pointer is `type *pointer_name`.

- **Pointer Initialization:** Initializing a pointer involves assigning the address of a variable to it using the `&` operator.

- **Dereferencing:** Accessing the value a pointer points to is done through dereferencing using the `*` operator.

- **Pointer Arithmetic:** Moving through memory using pointer arithmetic, where `ptr++` advances to the next memory location.

- **Arrays and Pointers:** The relationship between arrays and pointers, where the array name acts as a pointer to its first element.

- **Pointer to Functions:** Declaring and using pointers to functions for indirect function calls.

- **Void Pointer:** A generic pointer (`void *`) capable of pointing to any data type.

- **Dynamic Memory Allocation:** Allocating memory dynamically using `malloc()`.

- **Freeing Allocated Memory:** Deallocating memory with `free()`.

- **Pointers and Structures:** Accessing structures through pointers.

- **Pointer to Pointer:** Using pointers to pointers (`int **`) to hold addresses of other pointers.

- **Function Pointers:** Pointers capable of holding addresses of functions for dynamic calls.

- **File Pointers:** Pointers used in file handling operations with `FILE *` types.

- **Error Handling:** Checking for null pointers to handle errors effectively.

- **Linked List and Pointers:** Implementing linked lists using pointers.

- **Bit Manipulation:** Efficient bit-level operations using pointers.

- **Performance Optimization:** Strategies for optimizing code by minimizing unnecessary pointer operations.

- **System-Level Programming:** Pointers' significance in system-level programming tasks.

- **Best Practices:** Adhering to best practices for safe and efficient pointer use.